THE CONVERSATION OF DRAGONS

THE CONVERSATION OF DRAGONS

by

C. JoyBell C.

ISBN: 978-1536990546
ISBN- 153699054X

www.cjoybellc.com, authorcjoybellc@gmail.com

This is for the Strong, this is for the Learned, this is for the Magnanimous, the Innocent, the Burned.

PREFACE

From the day my beta reader team received this book in manuscript form, throughout the reading of it, up unto the end, their individual journeys have been what I can describe as distinct forms of: shaking, breaking, building, burning, rebuilding, reviving, reforming, transforming, transmutating, seeing, healing, decomposition and recalibration. Though their experiences have been unique to each of them as individuals, their respective paths while reading this work have all been one thing: *powerful*.

A beta reader team is a group of individuals that read the work before it has been published, in order to provide a preview for others, to give others a good feel as to what their experience with the work could be like or would most probably be like.

I first built my team on behalf of the book in *The Conversations* series that comes before this one, entitled, *The Conversation of Venusta*. None of them knew anyone else on the team I had pulled together, nevertheless, everyone warmed up to one another quickly and genuine friendships have been fostered ever since.

I am proud of my team; it is comprised of *very* accomplished individuals, leaders and shakers, as well as simple personas that bless the world with their gentle dreams and unassuming joys.

When I completed the writing of this work, I already knew that it was not just a book. Nevertheless, upon hearing the stories of my beta team members after handing over the manuscript to them, the realisation that this work is not just a book has become overwhelming. I began to recognise how I had breathed life into a living thing! I have taken a mound of clay and formed it into a living, breathing creature!

I continue to feel awe-inspired and I want you to know that you are not alone in experiencing events or circumstances that will be nothing less than transformative. If this is the Path for you, then you must follow through and finish what you are about to begin.

On the other hand, if this is not the Path for you, then you must not continue. We do not need to all share the same Way. It is a matter of finding one's Own. The value lies in what is your Own.

I can assure you that it is not at all my intention to sound mysterious, ominous or frightening. It is not a marketing technique, it is not a ploy. I am not trying to draw you in. You will be able to attest to this fact as you begin your journey. Believe me, the Magic within the covers of this book is not to be trifled with.

INTRODUCTION

The Conversation of Fire begins in a different way than how the previous books in *The Conversations* series began. *Fire* opens with a discussion I had with another person and is propelled forward by answers I gave to yet another person during a different conversation. Unlike the other books in this series, I was inspired to write this not completely through inner conversations, but also through discussions with other people. That is *not* to say that this whole book is based upon real-world conversations that I have had with a variety of people. Still similar to the previous books in this series, the gist of this book is moved forward by the discussions between my Inner World and my Mind. It is different, though, in that conversations with other people are what made me begin penning down the words and what encouraged me to continue with the construction of the manuscript.

I actually did not plan to release a third book in this series so soon. Between the first Conversation and the second Conversation, there is a gap of several years; so, I did not expect such an early release of a third book. This comes as a surprise even to me! Nonetheless, I felt pulled along — almost as if I was being dragged along — into constructing this book!

The building of this particular manuscript was unique of the lot not only because of how the writing began but also due to the fact that it is not written out from crucibles. For this, I am very thankful! If you have read *The Conversation of Venusta*, you will already know that I said I no longer wanted to produce writings induced by personal crucibles. I, in fact, decided that I would never again do it! In that light, I am very glad to be able to say that this book is produced in a completely different light as compared to the first two in the series. This one has been constructed more from observation and intuition.

Peradventure, I should say that the Human is morphing into the Angel, the gap between the two becoming smaller and narrower; this may mean that the 'reach' is shorter, less of an effort. Less of a distance to cross. Or, it could simply mean that I really have had enough and I was not ever going to write again lest it comes from joyous (or at least neutral) places.

I was torn between two titles for this book: *The Conversation of Dragons*; or, *The Conversation of Fire*. As you continue reading, you will see for yourself why I felt so torn between the two. Up until right now as I write this introduction, I am not certain which title to use. I could change my mind the last minute! I am going to leave this introduction exactly as I have written it and not come back into it to change anything, so, regardless of the title that I settle with, in the end, this introduction will remain as the open space during which time I was still deciding between the two.

Writing this series of books is a truly magical experience for me and writing this manuscript, in particular, has its very own uniquely esoteric process. I have noticed that when I go back into the pages to make edits and I remove a capitalisation or add a capitalisation— tiny changes like this— these have a palpable effect on the book as a whole! The book itself is like a river and the miniscule edits that I make are like stones that I am throwing into the river that cause ripples all throughout! I am telling you, that I can actually see and feel the changes to the vibrations running through the pages, every time I edit something. What does this mean? This means that this book is a construction of a structure, it is a house, it is a building, it is a bridge, a tower, a lighthouse! It is a physical object in the incorporeal realm. In the incorporeal realm, there are objects and structures which are physical there, but not physical for us here in our own corporeal realm. The incorporeal is in fact not always incorporeal! It is only incorporeal and intangible to us while we are here. One day, the tangible to us now will become intangible to us and the intangible to us now is what will become our physical reality. When we "edit" physical aspects of an object (like removing a nail or hammering in a nail), this affects the object as a whole. That is exactly how my edits affect my manuscript. I am left awe-inspired. What structure am I building? What does it look like? Have I seen it in my dreams, perchance? Have I touched it in my dreams, maybe? Maybe during travels to "the other side"? Is it a house? It is a temple, a tower, or a bridge? I wonder.

The writing within this book is meant to be consumed by those who have already internalized the two previous books in this series. Really, and this may serve as a warning to you, the contents of this manuscript will feel like walking on an extraordinarily narrow path, where the air from the abyss on both sides of you (left and right) are separated only by the narrowness that you are walking on! They are separated only by *you*! Two sides of an abyss and they mingle on the path that you walk on. You will find the words here come within a hair's width of making you feel absolutely uncomfortable (a hair's width of pushing you into the abyss, itself).

Reading the words on these pages will be like turning up some cups on your table, and to your astonishment, you find that underneath those cups—for all of those years, sitting right there on your own table— were precious, lost items that you had spent day and night searching for! The feeling is both a surprise, a regret (for not seeing what was under your nose all along) and lastly, a relief (for you have now finally turned your cups up to find those things once covered by them).

At times, you will feel threatened. Such is the case when you walk down a very narrow path in the middle of a great abyss; you would feel the threat of falling either way. You will feel that way at certain points in this book— only to be brought back to the comfort of the knowledge that the narrow path under your feet is there, is not going away, and is the *right* path to be on. This is all due to the fact that the great abyss you will walk through while reading this work, is not an abyss at all! It is the element of Chaos. At the end of this introduction, you will understand what "Chaos" means in the esoteric sense and you will see why walking through/with Chaos might make you feel such ways.

The work that I do is done half-consciously. Half of me understands what is going on and the other half is just as awe-stricken as you are. I know for certain that the process is actually not a simple one, and yet, the results are simple! Usually, we move from the scope of what is simple, into the arena of what is complicated. Contrary to that, my process moves me from chaos into simplicity. It's like going to the river of chaos and scooping up a cup of primordial stars there, then returning to my home and making tea out of that water! The tea is just another tea, but I, in fact, had to travel to the beginning of time to get the water for that tea!

What is chaos in this sense? Chaos in the sense of esoterism is not how we understand the word in the context of everyday life; rather, Chaos is the place where the laws of physics do not work as we believe them to work: where gravity, buoyancy, time, relativity, space and reality are not dictated by the laws of physics as we know them (if they even exist there in the known states that we are acquainted with). Chaos goes back to Original Power. A scoop of Chaos is a scoop of the moondust from the very first New Moon, the Moon before all Moons, the New Moon from before time began! And I do not mention the Moon in order to sound romantic, but I make reference to the first New Moon because according to certain writings brought to us by Mystic Rabbis, it is the measure of the beginning of the birth of Time itself. A scoop of Chaos is a scoop of probability: what if there is no Truth that exists in our sense of understanding what Truth is, could it be that Truth actually belongs just to the one who is able to scoop from the waters of Chaos, and then deliver

Truth however he/she wishes? Then *that* would be Truth— *that* would be what defines Truth. What if? In the place where no laws of physics apply and time and space are only as clay in the hands of the artisan, then Truth would come from the hands of that artisan because he/she would be the one moulding it!

Chaos within this book is not akin to burden, confusion or sorrow. Although, I wonder if those who are not ready for Chaos, would find it confusing and even sorrowful. Not to worry, I will prepare the tea as a simple tea. You will hardly even notice the difference. On the other hand, if you are not ready for Chaos, then please do not continue on this Path. You do not have to be here. Especially if your intentions are less than noble, less than innocent. Only the Innocent are welcome into the Dragons' Coves. May a dense blanket of irrecoverable blindness overcome the eyes of whoever proceeds on this Path with a heart filled with ill intentions towards me and those whom I love. May those not in possession of an Innocent Heart be led astray while reading this book and left permanently unable to glean of its Treasures.

If you are already familiar with Draconian Magic, you will recognise the Dragon Creed that I introduce on these pages. You will also notice the similarities between *my* Dragon Creed and the Dragon Creed handed down by word-of-mouth within some spiritual and enigmatic communities. As far as I am aware, this Creed circulates only via word-of-mouth within those select circles. There are similarities between my Creed and the Creed of old, but my Creed is certainly not identical to the other. This is not to say that I distance myself from the Creed of old, but this is just to say that I believe the Creed has evolved and that I am sharing the evolved version. I believe I am relaying a message for those on the Draconian Path.

In this light, I would like to point out that I am of the persuasion that Draconian Magic is too often exploited in modern times by practitioners of black magic or the so-called "lefthand path". While I am not saying that dragons should never be associated with those of the lefthand path, I am also saying that unfortunately the image of the dragon is exploited to that effect. I happen to be convinced that dragons are the Keepers of Treasure and that only the pure of heart are ever allowed near any of it! And when I say "Treasure", I am sure you already know I am referring to Treasure of all sorts; not only silver and gold (although there is nothing wrong with silver and gold). I believe that true Treasure is not going to be revealed to anyone not possessing a Pure Heart and it is in this sense that I also believe that it is my mission to bring the association with dragons into a newfound light: one that does not vilify them as belonging to evil. I am convinced that dragons are Keepers of the Pure and of the True Treasures.

If you are already familiar with the variety of my work thus far, you will be acquainted with the fact that I often incorporate animal symbolism into my books. *All Things Dance Like Dragonflies, All Things Lit Like Fireflies, Wolves of the Sapphire Sun*: These are titles of my creation that reflect the animal totems they are spun with. Dragon symbolism is not only about totemism, but it is far bigger than that. In the realm of animal symbolism alone, the dragon goes far beyond that and dwells in the realm of the most powerful. It is an "animal" (if we can even call the dragon an animal) that may encompass all other spirit animals because it is a shape shifter and because any animal would come to a dragon's call. Secret societies have been built around the dragon, brotherhoods have been forged, systems have been built and creeds have been given life— all with the dragon at their core. This is not to say that all of these systems, brotherhoods, creeds and societies are good, or are even similar to the dragon in nature. As I said, I see the dragon being exploited all too often in our modern era and more often that not, the exploitation is done by those who would wish to condone their own negative ways. On the contrary, such is *not* the nature of the dragon.

The conversation you are about to partake in will teach you the things that the Fire has taught me. I am a Fire Gazer and from the Flame I have learnt many things. I hope that this conversation will show you the way of my Dragon Creed. I cannot tell you that this will be an easy read, but I can assure you that I have written it all down in the simplest of words. Fire teachings are not easily understood by all, but if you *do* happen to understand, this means you are *supposed* to understand. Be ready to embark on a Path that I am sure you have never known before. Be not afraid, nothing can harm you here, as long as you wish me and mine no harm and hold within your eyes no envy.

If you ever need to dispose of this book, do not throw it into the trash; leave it on the branch of a tree or under the roots of a tree. Give it to the tree and then you may go on your way.

If you have not yet read the first two books in the *Conversations* series, please get ahold of those first before reading this one. I do not think it is safe to read this one before the others. It may be safe for some; however, since I cannot control who buys this book, I cannot know who may or may not read this before the others. With that said, I believe it would be safer for you if you read the others first.

This book is most easily described as an antediluvian-meets-modern work of thaumaturgy. On the one hand, we discuss archaic knowledge; on the other hand, we apply it to modern-day life and we discuss it in the context of our modern day and age. Though the content of this book is designed to build your Soul, Mind and Body, you will find it to be a solid reference to turn to for guidance on today's current, urgent world events concerning the domains of global politics and widespread social maladies. Community and its pressing issues, society and its pressing affairs, relations between nations and even the rise and fall of these nations are all delved into at a supramundane level. There have been books written to teach the art of warfare through poetry and books written to teach political ideologies through fairy tales and fables. This book has been written in order to raise a new generation. I do not mean a younger generation, but I mean a generation comprised of all ages. A generation that has been lost from this world for centuries, but now should rise again!

Older telestic and anagogic works written by the sages and mages of long ago have mostly been burned, or, are not very accessible to the average person. The average modern person living the cosmopolitan lifestyle laughs at the notion of mysticism and knows extremely little of the purpose for magic.

The highest form of magic is Soul Alchemy. Through Soul Alchemy, we transmutate the grotesque particles of our souls into the highest forms of gold. Physical magic is a lower form of magic, and yet, this is the only form that people today are familiar with. I deal with Soul Alchemy and this book will transmutate your soul, if it is the path that is meant for you.

Lastly, many have said to me that they read my books to learn more about me. While it is true that one cannot effectively separate the author from the manuscript, I would still like everyone to bear in mind that I would not like my manuscript to be transliterated as my actual diary or my own personal journal. It *is* personal, yes, but please do not think that I have blindly written on these pages without the foresight that potentially millions of people will read these words through the ages. It is therefore not my diary. Do not read this book to know *me*; rather, read this book with the desire in your heart to know *you*.

"If ever the Bush is on Fire hearken for the Voice and hear. Something is speaking — listen and listen— Something is shining— the Bush is on Fire."

— *The Philosophy of Fire*

"How can we heal people?"

"Human beings can heal and repair themselves as long as the corresponding energy that is needed, is around. People really don't know which energy they need to repair themselves with, though. For example, it is like having a medicine cabinet in front of you, but not knowing which medicine to apply to your wound... not all medicines are applicable to every kind of ailment. It is the exact same thing with the Soul.

Your friend thinks he needs the medicine of admiration. But I can see that what he really needs is the medicine of pity. Compassion. When this energy is around, he can begin to repair himself.

So the key is always to flow with the correct energy. And that is all. Even if a thousand people admire him, this will do nothing for him. Then if a single person flows with Compassion for him (not doing anything, just holding that energy within), this will heal him.

People are also like plants you see. They draw from the soil with their roots, from the sunlight with their veins, and from the water and the air. Same with people. Air, Water, Earth and Sun don't need to actually DO anything for the plant. They are just there, corresponding to the needs of the plant simply by being.

This world is filled with several billion people who are trying to heal themselves and who are striving to heal something else about this world, other than themselves. What you see in people's actions, are really wounded people thrashing around, trying to apply medicine to their wounds. More often than not, what they need to heal a wound or many wounds, is not the medicine that they reach for."

"Why is it that you are able to heal people?"

"That is an easy question to answer... I am able to heal people because I am all of the elements combined: Water, Earth, Air and Fire. Everything that a plant needs. And so when I am there, people heal, just as plants grow and repair themselves."

"How is it that you are all of these combined?"

"It is because I am the Philosopher's Stone. I am not a Philosopher, I am the Stone that Philosophers seek."

"How can we heal the world?"

"In order to change the world, you must first change yourself. In order to have the right to see what is wrong with the world, you must first earn that right through seeing what is wrong with yourself. We do not become influencers, leaders and teachers, through pulling on our better attributes and applying those better attributes to a broken world like a healing balm; rather, we become influencers, leaders and teachers in this world, by performing within ourselves the purging that we wish to see take place in others."

"Then how can someone become a better person?"

"It seems like such an amazing predicament to me, how one does not become a better person by seeking out in the world those who are lesser than himself and then saying, 'I will be better than you because you're not as good as me.' You don't become better by looking at others and trying to be better than them. You become a better person by looking at yourself in the mirror, and, seeking to overcome and to overthrow all the flaws within yourself, you overcome the weaker you, the lesser you; you become the better You, the stronger You, the higher You. That's how it goes."

"It looks like, in order to become a better me, I must see the Truth in myself, so that I may vanquish what truly should not be there, while at the same time nurturing what truly should be there. How then, can I see Truth? Or I suppose I should ask, *what* is Truth, so that when I see it I may identify it."

"Truth is neither good nor bad. Neither evil nor pure. It just is. Because through our convictions of good and bad, of evil and pure, we taint the truth with our own filters and our own desires. Truth is no respecter of what that man over there thinks is good or of what that woman over there thinks is evil. Truth remains as Truth, regardless of what you think about it.

It is amazing how *good* and *bad* are perceptions that change subjectively, depending on the person. Then there is Truth, which has nothing to do with either good or bad. It just is. What's amazing is how good and bad are merely perceptions of humans, and in reality, they are simply just two areas of existence; but then at the same time there are absolute rights and absolute wrongs. Rights and Wrongs have little to do with perceived "good and bad". The latter is highly subjective based upon individual personal perception, as influenced by religion, culture, and so on and so forth. Meanwhile, absolute Rights and absolute Wrongs are not subjective to these things.

There is an incredible amount of suffering in the world because of people holding onto what they believe is good, even though it is not the right thing to do in a given situation. You may think it makes you good, or a better person, but in the future, it will be responsible for immeasurable suffering. So ultimately what you've believed to be good and to make yourself good, is actually wrong, because the fruit of it is rotten. You will know a tree by its fruits, you see. Human beings cannot see the fruit before it grows on the branch and that is why so many failures occur in global society. But then how can you teach a person to see a fruit before it has blossomed on the branch of the tree? Is it possible to do that?

Judge not the tree until you know the fruit. The fruit is the truth of the tree. You may think your tree is good, but if the fruits produced are bad, then what you hold to be as good is *wrong*. If everyone were able to see this, then there would be no suffering in this world.

"Rights and wrongs. What things are these subjective to? Are they subjective? Can they be subjective? Who decides what is right and what is wrong?"

"Good and bad is a tree. Right and wrong is a fruit. The nature of the tree is ultimately determined by the fruit and you don't name the orange tree an orange tree until you see it bear orange fruit. So you may have an apple tree and believe it to be an orange tree and lay down your life upon your belief that it is an orange tree, but if the tree bears an apple fruit, what you believe about it doesn't matter at all.

Rights and wrongs are laws of nature. Goods and bads are fabrications in the minds of man. Of course, it would be Just to then name the right fruit as the good fruit and to then name the wrong fruit as the bad fruit, but the nature of the tree must bow down to the nature of its fruit. So name the tree after the fruit.

The problem here is that one needs to see the fruit before it is there and that is where humanity struggles. It is indeed very difficult for people to see what is not there yet. You could be doing something you believe with all of your heart to be the good, righteous and holy thing to do; but in the future the results of that are catastrophic. That, therefore, makes what you are doing now to be wrong, regardless of whether it fulfills all of your requirements of goodness! Or, you may be doing something now that you believe is bad, or that others believe is bad, but the future result of that will actually save countless lives from destruction. That, therefore, makes what you are doing to be right, regardless of whether it fulfills all of your beliefs in what it means to be bad.

After all, darkness and light are both simply areas of existence. And yes, there is a war between evil and purity. But this war is designed to bring out a single outcome. It is designed to bring out the Light. From darkness was born the Universe. From darkness were born the stars, the planets. Darkness gives birth to Light. The flame of a candle becomes evident in a dark room where there are no other lights.

That is why, for me, what I will call 'good' is what will cause life. Does something end in Life, in Beauty, in Light? This is good. Does something end in destruction, in darkness, in suffering? This is bad. Now the key is to know what the end is, while you are still in the beginning! This way, you will make the choice that is right and you will be able to call that right choice as 'good.'

To feed a rabid dog with your hand might be, in your eyes, an act of goodness. But if that act of yours results in that same dog biting your hand, you catching rabies and dying from it— that act is a wrong act. It has resulted in disease and in death. Is martyrdom good? I don't think so. There are many that will say it is good, but, I will not say it is good. I believe it is wrong, it has resulted in a loss of life, not in the blossoming of one."

"What of the man who lays down his life for his friend, or for his lover? Can this act not be called good and admirable?"

"The sacrificing of one's own life to save the life of someone whom he loves— this is an act of bravery— bravery is a necessity, it is neither good nor bad, it is a necessity. It is not a necessary evil, nor a necessary purity. Bravery is a Truth. And bravery done in Love is a Truth above all Laws. A Truth above all Laws goes beyond good and bad, right and wrong. It is a Law in itself, a Law for the True, the Beautiful, the Desirable, the Best."

"I can now see more clearly how to become a better me. But tell me, how can I help another person to become a better person?"

"You must always remember that we do not create Light by turning our faces away from those who are shrouded in darkness; rather, we become Light by illuminating the night. Let's say there is another person going through a dark night of his or her soul... you do not maintain your own Light by turning away from their darkness, but you become the Light, you embody the Light, by illuminating the night wherein they dwell.

There have been many who have said, that in order to create a dream, one must look only upon that dream and keep their faces away from all else—like horses with trainers upon their eyes. And I have told you here that in order to change the world, you must change yourself. Does this then mean that in order to change the world and make it a better place, in order to help other people to become better, we must then place those horse trainers upon our eyes so that we may only see the Light, the Direction, the Dream? No, that is not what this means. We change ourselves by facing our own nights, our own darkness— this is something that I have already taught you. In doing so, our Light is made evident. To do the same for another, is the same exact principle. Illuminate their night by simply facing it. It will not be your struggle, because it is not your darkness, it is not your night— but your Eternal Flame will glow in the very same way.

True and effective evil attains success through deception. Deception is the covering of true intention. An effective form of evil will never expose itself, its motives, nor its agenda. Not until that form of self, motive and agenda is already upon the people/ the other person. But then I believe similar can be said about Light and Goodness. You could say that the effective form of darkness is clothed in light; but you could also say that the effective form of Light is many times clothed in darkness. This is due to the very fact that darkness so wishes to cover Light, and a true Diamond from Earth is enveloped in rubbish. A diamond from the laboratory is never enveloped in rubbish; it is made pristinely by the hands of professionals who have crafted it with a specific outcome in mind. But then what is the value in that? The value remains in the Diamond from the rubbish. Rarely have I seen a person who says, 'I will be the goodness in the world', amount to what he has said he will amount to. How does Light get into dark places if it does not first clothe itself in darkened robes? How does one climb into a cave with not first bowing down to enter into it?

Furthermore, it is better to esteem others as better than yourself. Why? Because it is when you mistakenly esteem others as lesser than you, that you will be brought down low by your own shame. And it is better to rise slowly in the eyes of another than to present yourself immediately in all of your glory. Why? Because only a fool scatters out all of his riches onto the table in front of a stranger. A wise person reveals riches slowly as the stranger becomes a friend."

"Why shouldn't I rather esteem others to be equal to me, instead of greater than me or lesser than me? What about seeing all of us as equal? Is this not a better virtue than what you have suggested?"

"It sounds like the better virtue, yes, but it ultimately fails. To go out into the world with the preconceived notion that all are equal to you, is to prepare the ingredients for envy and arrogance. Because you will inevitably discover someone who has something that you want but you don't have; possesses a talent or a love or a home that you want but don't have. You will also inevitably discover someone who has far less than you, leading you to believe that you are superior; someone who possesses no impressive talents, fails miserably at love and does not even know where he or she comes from or is going to! You will inevitably discover those greater than you and those lesser than you; it simply will never happen that you will go out into the world and discover that all are the same. And so you see, if you were to make your mind comfortable with the idea that all are equal to you, this would result in you being first surprised by the truth, and then you feeling envy or arrogance. Very seldom will you simply feel acceptance in such a case, since you have already set up your mind to expect something that is not possible.

There will always be those whose presence makes you feel inadequate and inferior; likewise, there will also always be those whose presence makes you feel adequate and/or superior. The exception of this is if you are very empathic; because in such a case, you would feel inferior around those who are inferior and you would feel superior in the company of those who are superior: you would lose yourself in your company. That is not beneficial, either. What is beneficial is to know the truth about yourself, to regret what is flawed and to celebrate what is flawless. There are things flawed about you and there are things flawless about you. Regret one and then build anew atop its freshly bulldozed soil, change it. Then celebrate the other and enthrone it."

"I do not believe in having regrets. I believe that everything I have done, thought and said has led me to become the person that I am, today. Therefore, to regret anything I have done, said or thought, would be to regret where I am right now."

"You may speak for yourself. I easily regret many things. There are many things I have done, said and thought, that I regret! Whenever my actions have involved an unfavorable or a hurtful outcome for another person— those are actions that I have regretted.

I do not wish to take my actions that have hurt other people, or that have caused disappointment in other people and incorporate those actions like I would add feathers to my hat! The lives and the hearts of others are not disposable parts that add to my own life. Where the tip of another's nose begins— that is where the end of my freedoms also begin! And vice versa. Other people are not for the taking, for the pillaging. They are not feathers in our hats!

I have said things and thought things and done things, that I ought to have not said, thought and done. Why should I not regret what should not have been? I will regret such actions of mine and I will use the sting of regret to propel myself forward into a new change, a new direction, a new hope for myself. I will not stay stagnant in my pride, using my time and energy to prove that I have nothing to prove! I would rather simply say, 'I regret this, yes, I have regretted this deeply', and then spend my time and energy on changing myself, improving myself, becoming someone better; someone who would not do those same actions again.

Every day, I regret my flawed ways. Every time that tomorrow comes, the flawed way of yesterday is gone because I have removed it! I have become better.

In the world today, people look at the short term and when we look at the short term, we feel like we are moving on when we choose not to feel the sting of regret for our own actions. But in reality, I who have the ability to allow myself to feel the sting of regret will tomorrow meet you as a better person; while you will still be the same person, albeit the same person burdened with the need to prove that you have no regrets. While I would have actually moved past the regret by changing myself, by ensuring that I have turned from a caterpillar into a butterfly. You will still be stuck in your cocoon.

People of today avoid sting, avoid pain— they wish to fly with only one wing. They wish to only have pleasure and only laughter, they do not allow themselves to feel stung, to feel pain. But in birth there is pain. In metamorphosis there is discomfort. Now imagine yourself as a being that is capable of going through metamorphosis daily— a caterpillar that has the ability to change into a different kind of butterfly, daily! Does that not mean you have something more than others have? I think so. I think the caterpillar capable of daily metamorphosis has something more than the caterpillar that can only do this once!

Today, people believe that immediate satisfaction is a signal of good things to come. Instant gratification. But the truth is that instant gratification is not the prophetess of things to come. The absence of regret is not a tell tale sign of good things to come in the future.

Can you imagine what kind of a world we would be living in if all people were incapable of feeling regret? And can you stop to ponder upon what kind of world you think we might be living in, if all people easily felt regret for their own actions or lack of actions? Now apply this thought to governments, world leaders, leaders in your communities, societies and institutions. Is not regret the one thing that our world leaders lack? Can you imagine what it would be like if all leaders in this world were capable of learning from their regrets and becoming better each day? Can you imagine how much of a better world we would be living in right now?

You can also call regret, 'conscience'. With the decline of conscience, has come the decline of civilizations, cultures and creeds."

"Tell me then, how are we to love ourselves, and feel good about ourselves, if we are too busy dwelling upon all of our flaws?"

"On the contrary, I believe that regret does not dwell on flaws; rather, regret dwells on the fact that we may become flawless. Think about this: if there were no possibility of you to correct your own mistakes, then what would be the use in regretting anything? Regret in fact points to the fact that we are capable of becoming flawless. Or at least, we are capable of removing the flaws that we are able to remove. The sole reason why regret exists as a human emotion is for the benefit of the flawless parallel of yourself that is waiting for you.

It has been proven by scientists that there is such a thing as anti-matter. The exact parallel opposite of matter is an object of anti-matter. It is also true that the exact parallel opposite of anti-matter is the object of matter. Therefore, I believe that for every flaw that you have, or that you have made, there exists the exact opposite parallel of that. Without regret, you are left unable to see that parallel opposite. Regret is the sting that becomes your payment for stepping into the other parallel existence. It is the ticket you have paid, the token you have given!

I regret easily. But I also heal easily, I fly easily, I grow wings easily. Regret is the stinging cocoon that surrounds my caterpillar body; and I turn into a new butterfly, almost every day! We never stay in the cocoon! We turn anew!"

"What should I do if someone were to dishonour me?"

"People in this day and age— they are very strange— they dishonour themselves further after being dishonoured by another. For example, a man is dishonoured by his wife sleeping with another man and in return for the dishonour done to him, he dishonours himself even further by going around to every brothel in the city, having sex with as many prostitutes as possible. A further dishonour for an initial dishonour.

Can you imagine someone slapping your face, and then you using your own hand to slap the other side of your face after? Stupidity, right? And yet, this is what people like to do. They like to take the knife that was driven into their chests and stab themselves with it again and again; over and over.

I have experienced dishonour in my life, as well. But never think that I would dishonour myself further, just as what was first done to me! Each time I have been dishonoured, I have become better than the person I was at the time I was wounded. I have become the exact opposite of what they expected of me. I have never stooped down to their levels. Yes, I have made the mistake of stooping down to the level of others initially (as an initial reaction), but that is only an instantaneous and fleeting moment. I then spend the remainder of time on the matter, dedicated to enthroning myself. How do we enthrone ourselves? By emerging from the cocoon as a butterfly. We can regret broken relationships, broken friendships and less than beneficial initial reactions; but then we can quickly exit that cocoon and emerge far more beautiful than we were before!

I wait to see the day when a man dishonoured by a woman, turns around to the opposite direction and loves a different woman with a more passionate and fervent love, more than the previous woman could have ever imagined, dreamt of, or hoped for! I wait for the day when a woman dishonoured by a man, turns to face the opposite direction and pledges her heart to love a different man more fervently and more loyally than the other man could have ever dreamt of having! I look forward to the day, when the number of divorces a person has gone through, will equate to the number of times he has become more loyal, more loving, more caring, more courageous and braver than the last time! I look forward to the day when I see a man who has been heartbroken and divorced three times and instead of seeing a man incapable, I see a man who has grown three times stronger than before. I anticipate the day when I see a woman who has been divorced three times and instead of seeing a broken woman, I will be seeing a woman three times more capable than before! Three times stronger, three times kinder, more understanding, more open, more willing!

We are conditioned to the reality that pain closes us up and that is true, pain does close up our emotions and our minds. It closes up our hearts and our hands. But it doesn't have to be that way. We can change pain."

"We can change pain? Isn't that a very arrogant statement to make? For who can say that we can change pain? Pain has been around since the very beginning of time!"

"Pain is misunderstood. It is the worst thing to ever feel— I understand that— and that is why we misunderstand it. We hate it and nobody wants to pursue the understanding of what they hate. But I encourage you to change the nature of pain, not because I am friends with it, but because I am friends with you.

Pain dishonours us. We are often pained because of the fact that we are dishonoured. Dishonour pains us. But to take the knife of dishonour and to stab yourself in the chest repeatedly with it, is the greatest dishonour that actually occurs. Instead, take the knife of dishonour and stab the pain with it. It's going to be against your own instincts to do this, it will feel wrong and you will feel like you are not giving yourself justice— but I promise that you are in fact carrying out justice for yourself.

The next time— love harder. The next time— be kinder. The next time— trust deeper. The next time— give better."

"This sounds like you are being stupid. Like you are actually telling me to be a stupid person and never learn from my previous mistakes!"

"I would never teach you such a thing. Nay, we are to be wise as Dragons! But to love harder, to be kinder, to trust deeper and to give better— these can all be done with a renewed outlook, each time. A renewed form, each time. Just like how we, as a caterpillar, may turn into a new butterfly almost every day, we may also turn into a new lover, a new giver, a new kind of friend— each time we emerge from the cocoon! To love harder does not mean to do the same kind of love as before. It means to do a better kind of love than before. To be kinder does not mean to be kind in the same circumstances as before, but it means to learn how to be kind in a stronger way than before. To trust deeper does not mean to set yourself up for betrayal as you did before, but to trust deeper means to reach into the deepest caverns and ocean depths of trust—as deep as you can reach— where you will find the kind of trust that cannot be fooled, that cannot be blinded! And to give better the next time, does not mean to give and to give even to those who are not worthy of it, nay, but to give better means to give better also to a person who is so much better than the one before!"

"I understand what you mean… thank you… I should have known that you would never lead me down the path of stupidity."

"Oh darling, you make me laugh. You would do best not to doubt me, you would do best to trust me once in a while."

"How can we become better through regret, when after a mistake we no longer fit into the moulds that were first set? The butterfly for example… how can she become a better butterfly, again and again, when the first wings have been broken, the first cocoon been ripped?

When I look at families, for example, which are built upon a primary relationship between two people and then spun up into a tree branching out with many other individuals eventually springing from that one primary relationship— how can something like that be restored better after having been broken the first time, or the second time?

Surely, there must be a certain fixed mould that we should all come to expect? Especially from families? After all, families are the cornerstones of communities, which are in turn cornerstones of societies, which are then the building blocks of a nation! How then can we reconcile the image of broken families and broken people, to the hope of being better again and again?"

"I believe that no two families are the same. Because families are comprised of people, therefore, how can any two families be identical, when no two people are truly identical (not even identical twins). So why do we make a mould and expect other families and ourselves to fit into only one mould? The best kind of family is one that understands, empathises, communicates and feels one another deeply and on a daily basis. The earnest sharing of souls and hearts. That's the best kind. But just like how we strive to become the best kind of persons, we also strive to become the best kind of family. Furthermore, the person that we are and the family that we build, become intertwined. Ultimately, to make a family with your true other-half, with the other half of your soul, is the dream we all wish to have. So why not feel compassion for all families, everywhere? And lift them up as we also lift ourselves up. It's not easy, but we can all help one another and hope for the best for each other. No matter how many times a person has been divorced, that person can still find his or her true soul share. Life just isn't that easy, not all people get there the first time."

"So you mean to say, that I should not judge any family that I see and that I should not judge a man or a woman based upon their divorces and / or separations?"

"Yes, that is what I am saying to you. Life is difficult for individuals and life is difficult for individuals who come together and bring other individuals into the world, together. After all, inside each individual is a world. The coming together of two people is the coming together of two worlds. And then two worlds bring forth another or more, or many more! Some worlds come apart and then find another and then another… this is inevitable. I'm telling you, it is inevitable. I am not saying that it will happen to all; but I am saying, it will always happen on this planet that we live on. So we all have two choices: to remain broken, or to be born anew each time the cocoon rips open. We are born anew as individuals, as individual worlds (or, a part of us is born anew from these cocoons that I speak of), and as families we can also be born anew; with other people, with another person! The other option is to remain broken and to see ourselves as broken (broken on the inside and broken as a family). One choice will leave our nations in shambles and the other choice will lift our nations up and out of the trashcans.

Regret— and in your regret, enter into the cocoon of regret wherein you will remake yourself. Then reemerge as a newborn creation! There are few laws that are always as-is, very few! But of all the very few laws that stay as they are, this is one of them. Go through regret, allow it to propel you into the new creation that you are destined to become! It will sting, but the sting is what will give you immunity to what you have already experienced. I am not saying that nothing will ever hurt again and everything, later on, will always be wonderful. You might still get hurt and things may again turn sour. But it will never be the same, it will always be in a new way, with a new lesson that you may take away from it. And you will always be better than the last time. Always. I am not even saying that your circumstances will always be better than the last time; but I am saying, that *you* will be better!

I once had a friend who never got better than anything that he used to be. It was like being on the same exact day, sitting in the same exact sunlight, at the same exact time on the digital clock— nothing ever budging, nothing ever growing, nothing ever changing— it was like being with death! Indeed, there is a death that exists while one is still alive, and my former friend, he lived in it! And while I was still his friend, I lived in it with him.

This friend of mine would speak to me over and over about all of his mistakes; although, when confronted with the word 'mistake', he would never accept the word! He would immediately speak of all the reasons why nothing he ever did was a mistake, and about how grand of a mind he had! He wallowed daily in the exact feelings that are concocted by mistakes that one makes, yet without accepting that the source of his feelings was, in fact, the word: MISTAKE. He never regretted anything! And so he did the same things over and over again! Albeit, the mistakes were not identical, but they were all of the same nature, they were never new! Another mistake within another person, in another circumstance; nevertheless, it was never a better him and never a better counterpart and never a better outcome. It was always just the same!

If my then friend had been able to regret something— just for once— I believe that he would be a much better person today, living in a different day as a better person, with the hours on the digital clock actually moving in motion and not just stuck like that.

Actually, he did regret one thing in life. And he says that he lives with that regret every day... but I am not sure if what he felt was regret; or rather, if it was in fact guilt. We cannot live with guilt every day— that will destroy a person! Regret is different. Guilt is another thing. One can, in fact, feel guilty and yet not regret his or her own actions, on the basis of, 'Everything that I've done has made me who I am, today.'

To take that into context, let's say everything you have ever done has really made you who you are, today— are you sure that you really love and admire yourself so much, that there is nothing about you today which you would really never want to change? There are plenty of things about me I would be happy to change! I pray that I can change! I pray that I can heal and change and grow. I do not see myself as a finished product that could have never been anything greater or better than what I already am right now. I could have been greater, I could have been better. And I can still do that, now! And I can still do that, tomorrow. I still can."

"So your friend… he lived with guilt but without regret? And this, in turn, did nothing good for him?"

"Indeed, he lived with guilt, and yet, he would not change anything about the person that he was right then and there because he was convinced that we all ought to love and admire who exactly we are at any given moment. And so he was not even able to regret his guilt!

Regret is a proper funeral. Guilt is an open grave. Remember that. They are two very different things! To feel guilt without regret is to lie in an open grave with no tombstone, no friends, no flowers laying you to rest, no loved ones standing by your side… that is guilt. Regret is to be buried by friends and loved ones, with flowers laid upon the Earth for you, with a tombstone lovingly bearing your name and the numbers that mark your coming and going in this world. And then to arise— to arise is to come out of that grave and leave it empty! Worst is the state of the guilty man who has neither arisen nor been laid to rest!"

"Do you think that perhaps people are dictated by one?"

"What do you mean, 'dictated by one'"?

"I mean popular opinion, general mindset… influence over the masses…"

"Why of course. There always has been, and probably always will be, a method or many methods of controlling the mindset of the populace. In this day and age, I have observed that this method is by the way of self-righteousness. Tell the people that 'this' makes them a good person and then they will follow 'this'. Tell people 'that' makes them a bad person and they will shun 'that'. But then the branding does not stop there, it continues on in the way that they brand one another with the brands that have been given to them. They accuse one another, begin to find faults in one another, all in a bid to be the 'better person'. It is very easy to control the minds of people in this way.

People brand words and call the words bad. And yet, words are only writings on papers and sounds on tongues. People hate one another because of mere words. Kill one another because of mere words.

The only 'holy books' for me are the books that cause my Soul to bloom in Roses. Books are compilations of words, aren't they? Compilations of words that someone put together. A 'holy book' is a compilation of words that a person or that other people believe are holy. But the moment that a compilation of words causes me to look to my left and look to my right in order to see who is following my own standards— that is the time that it becomes unholy. *We are only defiled by the defilements that we find in others.* The defilements that we perform ourselves— those may be regretted, buried, fixed, or mended. But the defilements that you find in others— can you mend them? Can you fix them?

Can you regret them? Can you bury them? Nay, you cannot do any of this for them because they are not your own! Therefore, the defilements that you find in others become flaws you have taken upon yourself that you cannot wash away!

Stop to think about this, to *really* think about this. The defilements that are your own— these may be addressed. The defilements that are not your own but that you find fault in— they are not your own, but in finding fault in others, you have made them your own! And so, how do you ever fix what is really not your own? You cannot.

What is Holy to me, is that which can cause my Soul to bloom in Roses. If it causes me to become a channel of life unto others, if it causes me to become more understanding of others, to see pardon instead of punishment and mellowness instead of malice— then it is Holy. If a Dragon were to speak to me, and speak to me in words of burning flames— though everything I have previously known has taught me to believe that such a Dragon is evil— I will latch onto this Dragon and I will cling to this Dragon, if its words have caused me beauty, have caused me understanding, have caused me patience, have given me a better eye through which to see my fellow man.

We must see evil where it is, but we must not see evil where it is not. The problem with the religions of the world, is that it causes me to see evil where it is not. All of the religions of this planet are the same."

"Since all of the religions of this planet are the same, does this mean that it is all useless? The holy texts are useless, the scholarly articles are useless, the benevolence and the faith are all useless?"

"Of course not. The religions are the outer craftings created by societies and the ruling classes. But there is a life-bearing oil inside of those clay pots. The problem is that people are not breaking those clay pots. I am the breaker of clay pots and I have gathered the oils from within.

The oils are fragrant. They are of precious petals and of precious herbs. What will I do with clay pots?

I have no problem with clay pots and I will sit in any church if my friends bring me with them. After all, the fragrant oil here is the friendship; the church is the clay pot. In accompanying my friend to his church or to her church, I have become a better companion to someone that I am fond of and who is dear to me. This is the fragrant oil. Why should I refuse to sit in a clay pot with someone, if sitting there means I may unearth and bear the fragrant oil of benevolence and friendship?

And so, I will sit in any clay pot that my friend will bring me to. Especially if it is a very beautiful place! Yes, I like beautiful churches! The purpose of the church, to me, is the outer ornamentation of it. Because that's what it is— an outer shell. The more beautiful the outer shell, the more I will like it! As long as sitting there does not burden me. Now, if sitting there burdens me, then that is a different story, I simply won't go there."

"Tell me very plainly now, how does one find the fragrant oils inside the clay pots? This is all very good talk, but if one cannot simply do it, then how can it ever be done? If one is not you— then how can one do it?"

"Why are you so worried about this? You are me and I am you. It would not make a difference, anyway!"

"I ask not for myself, but I ask on behalf of others."

"It is very simple. To every religion, there is a mystical side, the esoteric side. Go to this side.

The side that people are on now— that is the exoteric side, that is the clay pot, that is the outer shell. The inner chamber is hidden, that is what we call 'esoterism'. It is what we refer to as, 'the esoteric'.

Remember that for every outer shell, there is an inner chamber. I once told you before that even in stones there is an inner chamber. Even the stones have voices! In all things, go to the inner, do not remain in the outer and by this, you will find the secrets of everything. Listen to the voice beyond the voice that you hear with your own two ears, it is those silent voices that will tell you secrets."

"Is that how you learnt all of your secrets"?

"Yes. This is how I learnt all that I know."

"You are telling me that to every religion there is an inner voice that cries in the wilderness, waiting to be heard?"

"Yes, that is what I am telling you. And all of this information is readily available. With some patience and with some perseverance, one can easily find the esoteric. Look for the mystical side of the temple. I am however *not* saying that I learnt all that I know by looking for the mystical sides of each religion, that is definitely not what I am saying. I have listened to the silent voices of all things, yes. Furthermore, there are the esoteric sides to each religion that they may seek out; that they *ought* to seek out.

Imagine it this way: it is like visiting an ancient temple built of archaic stone and upon inspection, you find many different symbols inscribed into the rocks every now and then, every here and there. These symbols all mean something, they are all hiding a meaning. If you have any spark in you at all, I am sure you would enthusiastically hunt down the meanings of the symbols that you have found in the stones. It is the same principle. Visit the temple but find what is inscribed onto it, because those are the bearers of secrets that are true. *Run with the symbols.*

Secrets are always true. That is in fact why they become secrets. Because the truth is often precious and bears a weight of great change! Often, the great change that would follow is something deadly for someone, somewhere. And so, the truth is kept locked in a secret. I suppose it is possible to intentionally craft a falsity and then to entomb it as a secret, but that is a different story for another day. It is also not very likely to happen. More likely to happen is that the Secrets inscribed on the Temple are the truths that you must find."

"How is it that you have been able to learn so much, to find so many symbols, so many secrets?"

"For me it is different. I hear the inner voice of all things. It is not I who seek them out; it is they who seek me out... some I have sought myself, but most has been given to me."

"Have you ever wondered, that maybe you know secrets because you are actually a part of the secrets?"

"I have wondered this, yes. And I know this, truly. Yes, I am a part of the secrets themselves, that is why I know them. To find me is to find secrets. And so, as you have found me on the inside of you, you have found all of these secrets that I have been sharing with you and showing to you. I am the oil and you are the clay pot, you were once broken open and out of the breakage, I have flowed! I am the fragrant Rose Oil and you are the Clay. In finding me, it just so happens that you have found many secrets. I am a part of many secrets."

"Which comes first? The esoteric or the exoteric?"

"The best example for this, so that you may understand it, is to look at the human being. The human being is both esoteric and exoteric. The human being is both corporeal body and incorporeal soul. Which existed first? Of course, it is the incorporeal that already existed prior to the corporeal. How can the mortal create what is immortal? It is the immortal that creates the mortal. Before your Body existed, your Soul was already there.

I do not say this is the same case for all of humankind. Many are born young in both body and soul. Never having been around before, they are babies born into this world. But I cannot speak for them, I can only speak for us, so let us not dive into what I cannot speak for.

Before the religions of the world were implemented, the souls of those very same religions were already dancing free. It is man who developed the need to encase the preternatural into a corporeal system easily grasped by the masses. And there you have it— religions of today as we know them!"

"Why was it necessary, or rather, why did they deem it necessary, to clothe the esoteric in an exoskeleton?"

"Because you cannot give Pure Fire to someone who does not even know how to hold up a torch. You must encase the Fire in a lantern and then teach the people how to maneuver the lantern, how to carry it and how to harness it. Without the lantern, the people will burn down themselves and the rest of the world, with the Fire.

Here is the strange thing: the strange thing is that it is not the Fire-bearers who created the lanterns for the people. Rather, it was those who were unable to dance in the Flames who were responsible for inventing the lanterns. Fire-bearers do not create lanterns."

"Are you sure about what you have just said? I know that there is a bigger Fire in you and you harness it with small words in a small book on small papers… is this not a lantern in itself? Be honest with me, can you in fact write this book in Flaming words, in full force and unfiltered? Is this not a lantern? Is this not a clay pot?"

"These are very good questions. But you will be happy to know that this book is not a lantern. This book is a wick. All flames need wicks to stand up erect; otherwise, flames would be running all over, unharnessed and unfocused. To create a wick is not the same thing as to create a lantern. I only need to light the wick, I need not teach a person to keep the Flame inside a lantern and how to carry the lantern and how to light it up and keep it lit. I have lit up my own wicks and you have gathered around them.

I bear Fire, and I create not homes for the Flames; rather, I give the Flames places to stand, places to burn and places where I may ignite them.

Now, if someone were to take my wicks, tie them inside of lanterns and then tell people a story of the lantern and how to carry it, then that would be entirely different and that would be what you are referring to."

"Would it be okay if people were to do this? Would it be okay if people were to house your wicks in lanterns? Would you let them?"

"My part is to light the wick, not to dictate where it goes. People will do as they wish."

"In order to master Flame, you must have also mastered darkness. Is this so? Or is this my imagination?"

"I have been wondering lately, you know, if darkness is not in fact imprisoned Light, imprisoned Flame. What if darkness is Light behind bars? This is a new thought to me, one that I have not really considered before... or maybe I have, but just cannot remember... what if darkness is Light in bondage? What if darkness is Flame in a state that we do not yet know of? We know flame to be a state that we can see and feel and sense, but we have not studied anything about a state of flame before it is seen, felt, sensed! But what if Flame does indeed exist in a prior state, whole of itself but simply unmanifested? And what if that is what darkness is? What if all darkness is still Light; only a different form of Light? Then it would actually make sense because all light in the universe was born of void, was born of darkness. Void is the source of the ultimate origins of life formation, because from void came forth the universe and everything in it. How could light have been born of void? How could light come from something that it is not a part of? Can Light be born of something that it is not already a part of? We have children and they are born of us, they remain a part of us for as long as they live. We ourselves came of other humans, remaining a part of them for our whole lifespans. We are a part of what we came from. What if Light is the same as Life? What if Light, too, just as Life, comes from what ultimately makes it everything that it is?"

"If what you say is so, then one could conclude that Void and Darkness are ultimately the sources of both Light and Life; or, are both Light and Life, in themselves!"

"Indeed. However, Darkness would be unmanifested Light and unmanifested Life. But it would also be the Void wherein the substance of both is already existing."

"Is this all so? Is this all true? This all stretches and pulls at my mind!"

"I am not saying that this is all so, that this is all true. I am only saying that these are the thoughts which have crossed my mind recently. And so, I have also pondered upon them."

"Do you think that you mastered Darkness in order to master Flame?"

"I do not know, I cannot say either way. Perhaps so, perhaps not. But I have truly known the feeling of Darkness running through my skin; there is a temptation of Power. And if my theories above are in fact so, this would mean that the temptation of Power which can be felt, is actually the potential for immense Light, for immense Life, running through the veins of Void and of Darkness."

"But if that is so, then it would mean that the ultimate form of Power is Dark."

"Not necessarily. What it would in fact mean, is that the ultimate birthplace of Light and Life is within Darkness. That doesn't mean that manifested Light and manifested Life cannot, with a single flame, outpower the Darkness from whence it came."

"I think that perhaps you *have* mastered Darkness. Because behold, you are not afraid of it!"

"They say that we need more Light; but I say that we need more warriors. Warriors are those who are not afraid of the Night. A warrior can stand in the Night and say, that the Night is but a blanket upon which are woven the cold crystal rocks we call stars.

There is no shame in your darkness, there is no shame in your pain, there is no shame in your loss, your hurt, your confusion and sadness. In all of that and in all of you, there is no shame. This world accepts only light and when you are shrouded in darkness you feel unaccepted by the light of your dreams, unaccepted by the light of what was and in the light of what could have been or what will be. In between all of these lights that we can see, there exists darkness of different kinds. I want you to know that though this world shuns that darkness, they are ignorant of the values of the night. In your darkness, you will find your Moon. In your darkness, you will find your Stars. In your darkness, you need not feel ashamed. All have their own darkness but they only show their light. So be not afraid. *Your darkness has a home.*

We live in a time where we see the light of others multiplied, expounded and placed upon pedestals. We see this every day on social media, the internet, television… we become disillusioned by these lights that blind us to the reality of acceptance for what we actually have. In between where we are and where we want to be; in between who we are and who we want to become— there is the reality of now. It is not an illusion. And the reality of now is okay. There is no shame in what is real. There is no fear in what is real. Know that you are okay. Here and now just like this, who and what you are— this is all okay."

"Who do you have in mind when you say these things to me? I feel that it is not me."

"Indeed, it is not you, but it is a friend of mine. She feels shame and she feels fear, because she sees the darkness that she is in and what she sees has found no acceptance in her eyes. What she sees has found no acceptance in the eyes of the world, either. The darkness that she sees herself inside of and inside of her, has no place in the world that she sees in her mind, that she wants to live in, in her mind.

We are told to use our minds as projectors, projecting upon a screen the ideals that we wish to become, that we wish to have, that we wish to hold onto— because it is only these images that have a place of acceptance in this world. Nobody wants gargoyles; everybody wants angels. Nobody wants sea dragons; everybody wants mermaids. The creatures of the Night and the creatures of the Deep are shunned, not accepted. When a person like my friend begins to swim and to fly with these creatures, she begins to feel fear, shame... she does not understand why this is happening when it is not supposed to happen! But it is this belief that there is no place for such creatures that is responsible for causing the fear, the shame. The more she sees, the more she shuns, the more she is afraid, the more she is ashamed. And then she begins to think that there is no place for her in this world— she shuts down, she closes down— there is no place for her Night in a world that worships the Day.

I want my friend to know that she has a home just the way that she is right now. Her darkness has a home. These creatures have a home."

"Are you the home of these creatures? Are you the home of Darkness?"

"If Darkness is the birthplace of Light and of Life, then I am the Home of that purest form of Flame called Darkness. But if it is not so— alas, we are not sure if this is so— then I am not home to it. But this I do know— that creatures both of deep and of dark, have a place in this world. They need not be shunned, they need not be shamed, they need not be feared.

Look at an image of the gargoyle. With its gnarled mouth and overturned teeth. Compare this to the marble angel. Who wants to fly on wings of a gargoyle? Nobody does. Who wants to fly on wings of an angel? Everybody does. But forgotten in all of this, is the fact that both angel and gargoyle fly all the same! Whether you have the wings of a monster or the wings of an angel— fly, all the same! Fly!

The darkness feels so unwanted and in turn, we begin to turn our backs on ourselves for having it. People don't like monsters. Gargoyles and Angels both have wings and can fly; but people only want Angels, not Gargoyles. Gargoyles don't usually have a home in this world; when we see them, we hide them and we persecute them! But we forget that we are supposed to mount them and fly with them, just as we would do with an Angel!

I want people to remember that they can mount up on wings of monsters, all the same; and learn how to fly through darkened skies with volcanoes blowing up all around them!"

"Is this why you are loved by so many? Because even their monsters love you? Do you welcome monsters?"

"I don't know how to answer this question. Yes, I am loved by monsters; I don't know if I necessarily welcome them into my own life. I do know that they are around and I don't persecute them, I don't shun them and I am not afraid of them. I suppose I am a creature of both Night and Day; both Gargoyle and Angel come and go at my call. And I think that this answers your previous question: Yes, perchance yes, I am a Master of Darkness, after all. In this particular sense, I am."

"Are gargoyles evil?"

"No, they are not. Evil is different. And I am now beginning to wonder if Darkness is in fact not belonging within the domain of Evil. For if Darkness is the birthplace of original Flame, then it cannot simultaneously be the birthplace of Evil. Life and Light cannot be Evil. But then there is undeniably a true form of Evil. We have always believed that this is the same thing as Darkness, but now I wonder differently. I wonder if Evil is not even associated with Darkness.

Consider the fact that Lucifer of the Bible was the Brightest Angel of All Light, beautiful in both form and function. And yet, he has now descended to the depths of all depths and the personification of all Evil, within the contents of the Bible. For such an embodiment of Evil to come from absolute Light; I believe is a signal that Darkness might not even be associated with Evil. Maybe it is just humankind which has made this association, for some reason.

And consider Hell of the Bible, for instance. We have read of this place, to be a place of Fire and Burning. Is not Fire the absolute primordial embodiment of Light? And yet, how could we have overlooked this for millennia? But alas, we *have* overlooked this simple fact.

If Darkness is the source of Evil, then why was Lucifer formed and turned in the presence of All Light? Moreover, why and how did that bright and shining Being come to then personify absolute Evil?"

"I am afraid of the things that you are saying, please don't say these things. Are you saying that what is Light is Evil and that in actuality, all that represents Light is actually Evil?"

"Dear child, do not be afraid; no I say no such things. And I will never say such a thing because that is not the Truth. As a matter of fact, one could say that if Light is the Child of Darkness, then Light returning to Darkness is only the child returning to its paternal origins. In such a case, everything would be Evil if looked upon through reference of Lucifer in the Bible. In such a case, all would be Evil and there would be no distinction between Beauty and Death. I say no such things."

"Then what are you saying? I do not understand."

"Perhaps Darkness is simply possibility. Possibility carries the potential for both Light and Night. For both Moon and Sun. For both Evil and Purity. Is the dark womb of a woman good or bad? Is the dark womb of a woman stained or is it pure? Neither. It is neutral; it is a receiver and a giver of that which it receives, but it cannot produce what has not first been given.

Darkness is perchance a Womb. The Womb of the universe, the stars, the planets, the galaxies… the Womb of you and of me and of they! And then Light is the manifested form, something that is born. But then Evil is, also. Evil is also a manifested form of what is born. Therefore, a Master of Darkness would be a Master of potential. It is not the Darkness which is Evil; it is the heart of the Master which holds either what is Evil or what is Pure."

"Do monsters represent those things that are Evil?"

"No, I do not think so. Monsters represent those things that are still in potential form. We do not usually like potential. We usually like to understand a finished form in front of us. We do not usually enjoy the wait; we usually want to have that which we are waiting for. There is an excruciating pain that lies in between the unmanifested and the manifested. We oftentimes find ourselves swimming within the unmanifested (that is, swimming in Darkness); while we swim, we see the Light on the other end, we see the place we want to be, the thing we want to have, the person we want to love... the things and people and places we have yet to know, or/and, the things, people and places we once knew. It is during these times that we are in the company of the Creatures of the Night. With Gargoyles. We seek out Angels to soothe us, but this is not the place of Angels, this is the place of Gargoyles. We utilise not their wings and this is a shame."

"If Gargoyles do not belong to Evil, then what are those creatures that do belong there?"

"First of all, I wonder where Evil is formed... I mean, where is the heart formed? And now, I am asking *you* a question! Where do you think the heart of a Master is formed?"

"The heart of a Master... I suppose these types of Hearts are different from others... I think maybe these types of Hearts were formed along with the forming of the other objects in the universe, such as planets and stars. Do you agree?"

"I suppose so. But then let me ask you about all other hearts, where do you suppose these were formed?"

"Maybe other hearts are born out of the influence of Masters... out of the influence that Masters wield through their actions spinning the silken spinning wheel of Possibility! A Master may spin beautiful Silk for long robes of freedom and honour; but then a Master may spin poisonous webs of captivity and deceit... other hearts are influenced, are created, by those who spin... am I right?"

"Yes, you are right. But then let us descend and go down lower, down into the level of the world that is around us— who are these Masters in an everyday sense?"

"I think that as we go down lower and into the level of this Earth, into our daily lives, we see Masters in the form of our parents, teachers, our guardians... we are influenced by either the presence or absence of Love that is given to us. Is this so?"

"Yes, this is so. You have learned well. And so, all are Masters in their own sense, for all have been given responsibility over someone else and over something else. All are spinning, although, the scale at which we spin is different for everyone. But all of these spinnings, no matter on what scale, are important nonetheless."

"So on a scale-to-scale basis, what we are witnessing are the Hearts that are formed from primordial substance itself; and then there are the hearts that are formed by those primal hearts; then after that, hearts that are formed by the hearts that were formed by the primal ones, and so on and so forth— have I understood well?"

"Yes. Hierarchy is not inequality of importance. Hierarchy is attention to detail. Remember this always. The mind falters and falls into falsity when it sees this Hierarchy as an inequality of importance. Rather, this Hierarchy is an absolute attention to detail. You need tiny needles to sew the more intricate embellishments on a tapestry and you need bigger needles to embellish the tapestry with more elaborate styles and forms. This is all attention to detail so that the tapestry may be truly beautiful in its final form. Without attention to detail, the tapestry is no good."

"Have you ever had a specific teacher? I know that you are going to say that you have learnt many things from many sources: human, animal, spirit, angel, so on and so forth. Even blades of grass and small flowers have taught you valuable lessons. But that is not what I am asking, I am asking if you have ever had the opportunity to learn from another person in the way that I learn from you? I *do* know that you and I are one in the same, but I wonder, did you ever sit down with a teacher, or walk with a teacher, a human being, who was able to teach you the things that you teach to me now in the way that you now teach me?"

"No. I have not. The search for a teacher was a yearning in my heart, one that was only fulfilled when I accepted the fact that I was the only one who could teach myself. That is precisely why I teach you now! Because you are me and I write because I teach you! This is not to say that I have learnt nothing from anyone or anything else; like you said, I learn even from the solitary blade of grass. But to answer your question, I say that no, I have not had the teacher that you inquire of.

At first, it pained me to discern the fact that I needed to become my own teacher, but after a long time, I accepted this Truth and let go of the struggle to find one. I think that even from a very fragile, young age, we all begin to look for someone to look up to, we begin to look for someone to admire above all others. We want to have a role model, that is how we are wired and it's normal. In that aspect, I one day realised that I needed to become my own role model, so I did. Now, in the aspect of having a teacher— I looked for one! I am not the type who does not like to be taught; I like to be taught! I am teachable. I am not complaisant; but if I believe you, I will ask you to teach me.

Not so long ago, I met an honourable Pagan High Priest named William, who used to live in Rome amongst the Pagan community there. He resides in Maine and aside from being a Pagan High Priest, he has also been a Wiccan High Priest for over twenty years now. I was not seeking out to become Wiccan, nor was I seeking a Pagan community to adhere to. It was not about finding a certain spiritual path, it was about talking to a knowledgable person.

There are many knowledgable persons, from many places: there are pastors, priests of the orient, bishops, missionaries, ministers, etc. But most of these other knowledgable people (if not all) are knowledgable on only one path, in only one creed (since they are adherents of their respective religions). I was not seeking to learn about any specific religion; I was seeking to learn just about Truth, just Wisdom, I wanted just Knowledge itself. This is why I asked him to teach me and oh did I have so many questions to ask him!

He told me, 'I cannot teach you, you must teach me. It would be wrong for me to teach you, the Gods would not approve of this, it would cause an imbalance in the cosmos if I were to teach you. I must be the one asking you to teach me. What is of Earth cannot teach what is of the Gods.' And I could sense an actual fear welling up in him, as if he were honestly afraid that the Gods would smite him simply for my asking him to be my teacher. This came after a very long time in my life, during which I yearned to have a teacher of knowledge, and it became a turning point. Right then and there, I knew I would have to either embrace what he was telling me and step up to fulfill my duties in this world; or, I could turn a blind eye to what he had just told me and continue to search in vain when I should in fact be looking into the mirror. I chose to step up and fulfill my duty to myself, to the Heavens and to the people. I chose to look into the mirror and become my own teacher, my own hero, my own friend."

"Who is God?"

"I believe that God is the Primordial Essence of Possibility. You can take God and do Good; you can take God and do bad! Alas, we see this everywhere! Good in the name of God and bad in the name of God. But Good and bad are ultimately the chemical makeup of the hearts that wield whatever is given to them. Give wicked hearts God and they will wield a sword of destruction; Give pure hearts God and they will wield a bouquet of roses! It is all God! But it is not all Good!"

"If this is so, then there is but one God for all of humankind; but demonstrated very differently by each!"

"If this is so, then there is but one God for all of the universe, actually. Then demonstrated very differently by all, yes."

"Does God demonstrate Himself differently, also? What I mean is, if people demonstrate God differently here on Earth; what are the chances that God demonstrates Himself differently throughout our planet or even throughout the universe?"

"I do believe that God demonstrates himself differently. After all, Primordial Possibility is exactly that: Possibility! Life is born again and again and in many ways! Why would not God express Himself in many different ways, languages and fables? Myths and Legends. Why not? Why would a God so powerful just sit on a chair the whole day doing nothing? Nay, I believe a God so powerful would be busy creating myths, legends and creatures of all kinds, all throughout the universe. Because, why not?

I believe such a God would have many children, with many names. Some of those children would be guardians of Lightning, others guardians of Spring... and still, others are guardians of Love and of Laughter..."

"What if I believe that there is only one God, with one Name, with one Language, with only one People. What would become of me in such a case?"

"If you were to believe that, there would be nothing wrong with it. And I would not tell you to stop believing that way. It would be simpler, easier and quieter. There is nothing wrong with simpler, easier and quieter. But be forewarned, that it would not necessarily be simpler, easier and quieter within yourself. On the outside, yes, you will have a church that supports you, people that are always on your side; but at the same time, maybe your heart will long for something more... maybe your heart will long to dance as God Dances, to express as God expresses… and then the quiet will be gone from your heart. If the quiet is gone from your heart, then I encourage you to follow the music to where it leads you. But if the quiet does not leave you, then I encourage you to stay where it is. If there is no music calling, then there is no music for you to follow."

"But you *do* know that I have already followed the music, don't you?"

"Of course, my child, for you are I and I am you."

"You must be heavily-laden with armours, aren't you? For someone to be unafraid of monsters, surely she must be clad in iron and silver! A true knight from head to toe! What games do you play, what tactics do you employ; show me your pieces and your cards, the pieces on your board and the cards up your sleeves! Show me, so that I may also become Master of Darkness. So that I, too, may one day speak so eloquently of God!"

"I have no pieces and I have no cards. I only have armours but they are worn and rusty by now. My armours I have worn in the place of my absence of pieces and absence of cards. I sit with the Dragons, and with a Dragon's heart I feel the pains of the games that the humans play and the tactics that the humans play... everything human so easily hurts me. Even the human love, the way they say they love but it doesn't feel like love to us Dragons. That hurts me. We have no cards up our sleaves because we wear no sleaves. We have no pieces on our boards because there are no boards! We have armours, because if not, the people will hurt us.

We only have flowers. I have a table and it is laden with flowers. Some show up to my table clad in armours and covered in sleaves and bringing their game boards. But my table is only for flowers. It is set with flowers. I have only flowers."

"How can it be? How can it be that someone like you can talk with the Dragons and Master the Darkness? How is it that a Flower Bearer speaks in Dragon Tongue and calls the beasts to come and go as she pleases?"

"Oh but did you not know, child, that it is *only* those like me who can? The way of Purity is very narrow: straying to the right hurts and straying to the left hurts even more. So the path of Purity walked is narrow and on a very high ground. Did you not know that on this high ground the flowers grow and the flowers are picked? Did you not know, child, that even monsters like flowers?

But humans are different… humans do not always want flowers. They want the one who wins the board game and they want the one who plays the cards better. That is almost always who they want. They do not usually want the one who bears flowers. And when I go down to the place where they compete and they play— my heart aches and my skin hurts! I used to think that they were hurting me, but then I realised, that the pain came from the fact that down there it is made up of an air that my lungs cannot take in! Down there, it is made up of an atmosphere that causes my skin to melt away! I do not hurt because the humans hurt me; but I hurt because the atmosphere is not my own and I begin to disintegrate. Therefore, in order to heal myself, I simply return to my atmosphere where I breathe my air and I bask in my own Sunlight."

"So you are saying that you come from a place of Dragons and of Monsters; of Angels and of Light; of Gargoyles and of Gods. It is a place all Pure and that is why you are not afraid of the Darkness; it is not because you are well-equipped with weapons and with venoms that you are Master."

"Yes, that is what I am saying."

"How pure are people?"

"Their Monsters run to me. Their Angels run to me. I see their Monsters and their Angels. Do I see *them*? I am not sure. It is hard to see humans because they are covered up in so many skins and then in so many clothes and then in so many armours. Are people pure underneath all of that? Who knows. Only God knows."

"What *is* evil?"

"I believe that evil is superficial charm. I know, that does not sound like what you have always thought evil would be like. But I believe evil is superficial charm.

Look at it this way: if Darkness may be the Deep where all Possibility is conceived; the birthplace of Flame itself (and Light, that is), then evil cannot, in reality, be a part of it. This would then mean that evil cannot belong to what is Deep. That would, in turn, mean that evil resides in the shallow. That is not to say that all which resides in the shallow is evil, or that all which resides in the shallow is associated with evil. Not at all.

What is responsible for leading the masses astray? Superficial charm. What is responsible for you and I being deceived in life? Superficial charm.

What do murderers use to catch their prey? Superficial charm."

"What is superficial charm?"

"Superficial charm looks pleasing on the outside; it tickles the senses; it appeals to the lower registers of the human being; it attempts (and oftentimes succeeds) at bypassing an individual's foresight, insight, wisdom and intuition."

"And this is the face of evil?"

"Yes. This is the face of evil."

"What kind of a creature can overcome evil?"

"We are Dragons in this world. We have only eyes for the Original Flame, we burn away every superficial charm. The Dragon is Keeper of the Flame; the Dragon is One with this Flame and this

Flame burns away all superficial charm. The Dragon *sees.* To be a Dragon is to *see*, to have Dragon Sight. The Flame overcomes the evil. The Dragon overcomes the evil."

"What does the Dragon see?"

"The Dragon sees Purity of Heart. The Dragon guards its treasure from all but those who are Pure of Heart."

"Do you think that Purity of Heart is the ultimate opposite of evil?"

"Yes, I do think that. The ultimate opposite of superficial charm is Purity. Purity is represented by the Dragon because the Dragon *sees*. To see is to not be influenced by the effects of superficial charm. The only way that superficial charm can work is if you are unable to see what is beneath the surface. Therefore, evil is effective upon those who do not see, while those who see are Pure. The Dragon is Pure."

“What is the Flame like? What can the Fire teach us? What has the Fire taught us?”

“The Flame is soft, it dances, it twirls around and it leaps up and bows down… it is never afraid to bow down. It is equally unafraid to stretch itself up high and reach! But as unafraid it is to reach higher, so is it unafraid to bow down lower. It is soft, it gives way, it adjusts, it does not impose itself. It is very different from water. Water imposes itself, it cannot be captured in the hands; it will run through the fingers. Water will drill holes in rocks and overturn mountains. Water also hardens— this is something that Fire never does. Fire never turns to ice, never hardens. Fire flows in a way that water does not flow. Fire is humble. They say that Fire roars, but I tell you, that Water roars louder than Fire!

Much good has been said about Water, but let me tell you that when I was made of Water, I hardened at the gust of cold winds! I hardened and I turned to ice. My Mind was disturbed and out of my control. But the Fire— the Fire contains me, it contorts as my Soul contorts, bends as my Soul bends, sways and flows as my Mind flows! Fire is centered because that is the nature of Fire. It is centered on a wick, it is contained and yet it is Free and Powerful!

The Power of the Fire is in its softness; it does not need to harden in order to overcome. In fact, by nature it is soft and all it touches becomes soft, as well. Nevertheless, the Flame may grow and rise and overcome all in its path without hardening. Still, it bows and it rises, it sways and it dances to its own music, to its own song."

"I thought that Fire was harmful, I thought that Water was soothing and gave life!"

"All of the elements may become harmful and all may become helpful. That is not the question to ask. The question to ask, is, *which element is my own?* Because the element that is your own, is the one that will not be harmful to you. Water was harmful to me, that means it was not my own. Fire is not harmful to me, that means it is of me and I of it."

"Is there a lesson that the Flame may teach everyone? Because from what I can see of what you are teaching me; the elements are very personal, they apply to each individual as per what the individual is comprised of. But my question is, *is there a lesson that the Flame can teach the general public*, regardless if they are even comprised of any element or not? Regardless if they are newborn Souls or ancient Ones? I ask this, because wouldn't it be great if all could learn a lesson from the Fire, from the Flame?"

"You ask this because to learn a lesson from the Flame would be to learn a lesson from the primordial material that is elemental particle to my Soul."

"Yes, that is it."

"Yes, there is a lesson for all. It is in the form of the Flame. If you take a candlestick and light the wick, you will see the form of the Flame upon the wick. There is an Outer Flame and there is an Inner Flame. To extinguish the Outer Flame is to extinguish the flame as a whole. One cannot say, 'Both the Outer and the Inner are the same and the Inner exists for the benefit of the Outer, so that one day the Outer may become one with the Inner and on that day we will all be the same.'

To say this is to extinguish the entire Flame, and I tell you, this has been the cause for every downfall of every advanced ancient civilisation on this planet. Observe the fall of the powerful Atlantis, of the powerful Egyptian Kingdoms. They collapsed when the Outer Flame fell into the Inner Flame and all became dissolved. The Outer Flame must be maintained, just as much as the Inner Flame must be.

The problem with the human race lies in the fact that people want everyone and everything to be the *same*. 'All is One' they say. Their understanding of *All is One* is the hopefulness of a simpleton, but it is not the TRUTH. They have not understood the TRUTH. Yes, All is One as the parts of the Flame are One. But the parts of the Flame are not the SAME. *Same* is not the meaning of *One*. I have taught you this before, I have shown this to people before, in different ways and using different pictures, words, explanations. Though the pictures and the words vary; the message is the SAME— that we should *not* strive to be the same. The only thing that is the same about all of us, is the fact that we are not the same.

This is the lesson of the Flame— that if you attempt to make the Outer into the Inner, then the structure will collapse and the Flame will be extinguished. When you extinguish a flame on your candle, do you keep in mind to put out only the outer or to put out only the inner? Of course not, you simply put out the flame. But what part of it is removed first? The inner or the outer? Of course the outer. So what happens to it? It has collapsed into the inner and without this outward structure, none of the flame may remain!

The lesson is very simple when applied to the Flame (not only the everyday flame that you are well acquainted with): our lots in life are occupied by us because those lots have a use for us. The problem arises when a man covets the lot of another and attempts to bring the other down so that he may overthrow the other's lot in life. The unfortunate thing is that this is, in fact, possible. The Outer, seeking always what is Inner— because he believes that all must be created and must exist for his own benefit— is capable of overthrowing the Inner. We have seen this in the fall of the Greats. That is why it has been said, by some of the greatest hierophants of yore, that our Inner Flame must be kept hidden within a treasure chest of their own disbelief because that disbelief will be the Keeper of the Inner Flame, guarding the Inner Flame, thus keeping the whole structure alive and well in order to avoid implosion."

"Are you saying that we are not all created equal?"

"Equality is an overused word that has become something like a vampire, sucking on and thriving off of the emotions and frailties of those who use the word. Forget the word 'equality' and instead, think of the word 'sameness'. What I am saying, is that we are not created in sameness!

Lucifer was of the Highest Order of the Outer Flame, an Angel who led all of the others! A bright Angel of Light and of Music! Still, there came a time when he came to covet the Inner Flame, believing that all must exist for his own benefit, that all must become ONE. And now… let me stop for a moment to encourage you to really let this sink in… you must realise the nature of evil carried within the misconception of the phrase *All is One*. The misconception of this is, in actuality, the very poison that ran through the veins of Lucifer. In thinking that all was 'One', he interpreted this as meaning that all must be 'Same'. When in fact, the only reason that *One* can exist, is due to the fact that *not* all is *Same*! Once the Outer Flame and the Inner Flame are moulded into sameness— they both cease to exist!"

"I can see clearly what you are teaching and showing me, your words are simple and they do not function by twisting current knowledge… I am most alarmed by this…or amazed, rather. I am amazed by the fact that you are only pointing out exactly what everybody already knows, but why is it that when you point it out, without even twisting the story, everyone is able to immediately see what they did not see before? But they were looking at the same thing you were looking at, all along!"

"That is simply how nature is. Two individuals may look upon the same exact thing, but see two totally different stories!"

"I already know that, but even that is not the explanation of what you are doing. You are not telling a different story, you are telling the same story; but for some reason, when you tell the same story, another can see and understand something that they did not see nor understand before!"

"Alas, this is the nature of Fire, you see, the Fire may look upon a vegetable and see a stew; the Fire may look at a tree and see a pile of ashes; the Fire may look upon a cow and see a feast. The Fire looks upon the same thing, the same story, but gives you something else."

"If so, then Fire is not evil! Because if you are of the Fire and you are able to open the eyes of others to Heal, to Comfort and to Love, then you are not of evil! And if you are of Fire and you are not evil, then Fire is not evil!"

"Fire is not evil. We were taught since our youngest years that Fire belongs in Hell and Hell is the place of weeping and gnashing of teeth... but is it not Fire that feeds? Is it not Fire that polishes and causes objects of value to shine? Is it not Fire that gives warmth on a cold day or a cold night? Is it not Fire that may destroy one's enemies?

We may say similar of Water! Is it not Water that quenches thirst? Is it not Water that washes and causes things to become cleansed? Is it not Water that brings comfort on a hot and humid day or a hot and humid night? Is it not Water that destroys one's enemies?

And so you may now see, that all elements are able to give life,to soothe life and to take life away! And remember that in the story of Hell, the fire there does not dissolve anything. It is therefore not the pure and original nature of Fire. It is not actual fire. The fire of Hell does not turn anything to ashes, does not incinerate anyone or anything there! They live on, still! Unaffected by the flames! The fire in Hell could be easily replaced by water that cannot drown, or air that cannot give life to the lungs, or rocks continuously falling upon heads that are unable to break! And so you see, Fire does not belong to Hell. That is a different thing that is there.

Of all the elements, Fire is the one which can look upon something and see something more. We cannot say that Water looks upon a tree and sees a log cabin, we cannot say that Air looks upon a person and sees a bird, we cannot say that the Earth looks upon a cow and sees a diamond. And so you see, that attribute belongs to Fire, to Fire alone!

What is happening in Hell? In Hell, Fire is stripped of its attribute to look upon something and to see something more. All are left the same in Hell, and yet fire burns still. It is Hell when fire is not Fire, when Fire is stripped down to nothing. *That* is Hell!"

"But wait, can't we say that Water looks upon a tree and sees a home for birds and animals? Or that Water looks upon a tree and sees a shade for the man? And can we not say that Air looks upon the lungs and sees life in the human? And maybe Earth looks upon the cow and seas a living thing worth nourishing. Can we not say all of these about the other Elements?"

"You have a very good point! The other Elements may also look upon a thing and see something more. Perhaps Air looks upon the unborn child and wishes to fill its lungs; perchance Water looks upon a seed and wishes to see a flower; happenstance Earth looks upon that same seed and wishes to offer itself as an anchor. Through Air the child may grow into the one who picks the flower to smell its aroma, standing under the Water that drips from the clouds and the Earth will feel the pull and the breaking of the stem it has anchored! And so, they are all connected, are they not?"

"Yes, they are! Does this mean that what you just told me is wrong?"

"You could say that what I just told you is wrong if you are not looking at the Elements through my eyes. But when you look at the Elements through my eyes, you will then understand what I have just told you a bit earler.

Fire is the Element that is not processed in order to exact a result; rather, it creates the process, it is the cause of the result. For example, Earth transforms into nutrients for the cow; Water is processed through photosynthesis into rain; Air transforms into different types of air masses and different types of gases, each of the transformations having a different effect, for a different purpose.

Fire is always Fire, you see. We may harness Fire in many ways, but the initial essense causing the effect upon the thing, is always the same Element in its purest form. There are many objects that are flammable, but they themselves are not fire, they are merely flammable.

I can explain even further: Air may create ice, by changing temperature and freezing Water. Water may grow trees, by being transformed by the Sun during photosynthesis. Earth may give nutrition, by transforming into nutrients within the living body.

Fire is always hot, it always burns, an interference with its pure state would cause it to be no more. Fire does not become cold, it does not transform into a different bodily structure, even the Sun itself is still the pure form of Fire: the Sun is Flame! Unlike Air, Water and Earth, Fire cannot be polluted. How would you pollute Fire? Fire would rather be extinguished than be polluted. Or, it would burn away whatever attempts to pollute it!

Light a Fire in the dead of winter, will it freeze or change its constitution? Or will it burn just the same as before? Will it fail you in the dead of winter, or will it provide for you just as it did before and just as it will, tomorrow? If you light a Fire in the dead of winter, when the Air is harsh, the Water is frozen and the Earth has fallen asleep, will the Flame fail you? Will the Flame abandon you? Will the Fire say, 'all have changed, I will also change' and then cease to bring you warmth? Or will the Fire say, 'all have changed, but I will not change' and then burn brightly with the same candour as it did before and as it will continue to have long after the winter is over?

I hope now you are able to see how Fire is set apart in its purity. I have not told you that Fire is superior to all; but that it is set apart from all. This does not diminish from the beautiful story of the infant who became a man, who then picked the flower under the rain, plucking the stem from the Earth! That story is not diminished in beauty. There is no competition."

"I want to learn so much more of the lesson that Fire has to teach; I want to learn so much more about oneness and about sameness. Show me more, teach me more about this."

"There is a lesson urgent in current times, having to do with issues between men and women. There is a struggle between the two sexes, a struggle which is entirely unnecessary and totally at fault for a great deal of damage in the world. This struggle is entirely unnecessary because every female on this Earth came from the loins of both man and woman, every male on this planet came from the loins of both a woman and a man. Neither sex would exist without the other and yet, there is a struggle for power and for sameness. Again, to be 'one' is not the same thing as to be 'same'. Though a man and a woman become one, this does not mean they must be the same. In fact, they are not the same; they are in fact complimenting particles of one another. Things that are the same cannot compliment each other; rather, what is needed to compliment anything, is something that is different.

Why is there such a struggle to be the same? Women must do as men do and men must do as women do— this is not needed— this creates imbalance. To eradicate manhood is to eradicate womanhood. In the case of men and women, a woman is the Inner Flame while a man is the Outer Flame and as you already know by now, to eradicate the Outer is to do the same to the Inner. Women must not seek to eradicate manhood and men must not seek to eradicate womanhood; to do so would be to eradicate the self. If we were to eradicate one of the sexes, we would be eradicating both sexes.
Let's say one day in the future, they will find a way to produce humans without the need for the sexes, in that case, let me ask you, which sex would they choose to make all humans in the image of? If future humans will all be bred in test tubes with no need for an egg and a sperm, there is still the question of whether or not the embryos created will be one sex or the other! Sexless humans are not humans. Sexless humans are robots, are Artificial Intelligence, are

post-humans. In that case, we would be talking about an entirely different species.

There is another symbol of oneness which is actually the symbol of both sexes and we call this symbol the Yin and the Yang. This is the intermingling and the interdependence of the feminine energy and the masculine energy. This is duality, this is the sustainability of the universe. Ying and Yang is the universal symbol of sustainability. As Yin swells in size and in height, the Yang begins to emerge. As Yang swells in size and in height, the Yin begins to emerge. Each compliments the other and helps the other to rise up. Furthermore, within the Yang, there is a bit of Yin and within the Yin, there is a bit of Yang.

Look at you and me! You and I are this duality, you and I are Yin and Yang! This is why we have these conversations. Without the duality and without the balance, we would not be having any of these conversations! We are Yin and Yang— You and I!"

"Does this Inner-Outer, Yin-Yang, Philosophy of the Flame— does this apply to other areas and not only to the balance between male and between female?"

"Yes, of course. This is applicable on the massive scale of human societies coexisting on this planet. They will tell you that the goal of the Outer is to become the Inner (as they have been telling you for millennia); this is the reason why ancient and great civilisations have fallen time and time again, then humanity begins to start anew. How many times has civilisation of humankind fallen and begun again from scratch? Many times! Still, every single time, the very same lie arises and is aroused in the hearts of many: the goal that all must strive to become same, all that is Outer become Inner. And as I have already said, to extinguish the Outer is to extinguish the Inner. To extinguish the Inner is to extinguish All.

How many times has All been extinguished? Many times! Humankind is indeed powerful: powerful enough to extinguish great and mighty things. Power that is deceived, is power that will produce destruction. Power in itself is neutral; when it is mixed with lies it becomes hazardous; when it is mixed with Awe and with Reverence, it becomes Fruitful. The greatest goal of attainment for Power, is to become Fruitful. Fruitful, that is, bearing beautiful fruit! Not bearing rotten fruit. Rotten fruit is in fact not bore; rather, rotten fruit is what becomes of fruit when mixed with deceit, with lies.

Many a time has humankind been lured with the promise of 'equality' and 'oneness'. These words in themselves are neutral; but when these words are injected with malaligned passions, these words become destructive. Hence, there has been the destruction of civilisation over and over again. This fall of civilisation always occurs at its height, why do you think this is so? Is it because God strikes down those who ascend to heights belonging only to Heaven? Nay. It is because as humankind ascends, the vision always becomes unified and then this unified vision becomes the core of destruction. You would think that unity is what will heal a civilisation; and to a certain extent, this is true. But there must be a unified acceptance of the knowledge that all have their own lot in life and the lot of one may not be the lot of the other. Most human beings are born with covetousness in their hearts and I tell you, covetousness is the root of all evil."

"What is evil?"

"As I have already told you, evil is something that does not appear as it is. You can witness that as superficial charm in its resting form; but in its active form, you need to see this as the hand of covetousness. There is no greater evil that exists, than that which is able to show you a different reality than what is your own. There is no greater evil that exists, than that which is capable of stripping you of your worth in your own eyes.

You lived in a castle, yet you only saw a straw hut. You were draped in precious robes, yet you only saw torn rags. You were loved, yet you felt unwanted. I tell you truly, that there is no greater evil that exists, than the evil that is able to strip you of your Truth, of your Joy, of your Delight.

Imagine yourself as a child, receiving a beautifully-wrapped gift and in that gift is the thing that you most longed for, in pristine condition, new and untouched— designed specifically for you! Then imagine the voice of an envious onlooker whispering into your ear from behind: 'it is broken, it is not the right colour, it is an old thing that nobody should want, it is dirty, it is something that nobody else would want.' Then imagine your vision of your gift changing and morphing to meet the descriptions of the voice that has whispered in your ear! It is the voice of covetousness, it is the voice of equality, it is the voice that does not want you to have what it does not own. 'Equality' as understood by the mind of the simpleton, does not want anyone else to have what it itself does not have. And the greatest— I tell you the greatest of all tragedies, is when you are persuaded by that voice, fully live the descriptions of that voice and go on in life as if the gift is not there, as if you do not want it, do not see it, do not need it; as if you are just like the one who whispered into your ear! I tell you, that there is no greater tragedy than this!

There are many born with no eyesight, no hearing, or with many other forms of disabilities. But they know their truth and they live in it. Suffice to say, they live their truth. Greater is the tragedy of the human born with many good gifts, who sees them not, who hears them not, who perceives them not; and instead, takes on the perceptions of the one born with no eyesight, no hearing and the disabled. This human does not live in truth; this human lives in deception caused by covetousness. Therefore, I say that covetousness is the root of all evil. Evil is a lie, a deception, a robber. If there is a devil that exists, I tell you, this is it! The force that has the ability to make you see your castle as a straw hut and make you see your precious robes as torn rags— this is the devil!

Can you imagine what it would be like for a person to die and then to wake up in the next life, only to realise then that their straw hut was, in fact, a castle and that their torn rags were in fact silken robes? Only to realise in the next life that their bitter rejection and unwantedness were actually open arms of love waiting for them to respond? Waiting for them to *see* they were loved all along? Can you imagine the frustration of the one who has died and passed over to the next life, with eyes no longer tainted, no longer deceived, only to see the treasures and the many beautiful and good gifts they owned while they were still alive, after that life is already over? What utter frustration! What utter anguish! What *utter* pain! So much frustration, anguish and pain that the individual would cry out and say, 'send me back again and this time I will not be deceived, I will not be pulled down, I will live the life I was meant to enjoy!' Now, if they are able to live the life they were meant to enjoy the second time around—

I cannot answer that. But if not, oh what a doubled frustration that would be!

I know that you think, that envy is not powerful and that surely you cannot be pulled down by the covetous hands of 'equality'. But mark my words, humans have a power in this area. It is the super power of the ordinary human being! A power so great, it has been able to equalise opulent societies into nothingness, time and time again. Covetousness seeks to create a universal form of equality and it enacts upon this desire by pulling down those who are above, onto a lower level that the rest are built upon. You see the devil every day in varied forms. In the voice that whispers into the ear of the child opening the much-awaited gift, in the voice of jealous and lacklustre co-worker, in the envious glances of those who surround you... these are all forms of the devil."

"Surely, there must be a true form of equality that is not evil in nature? Because if not, then you would be saying that those who seek to end inequality in the world, are devils!"

"Those who seek to remove inequality in the world are not evil in nature. And usually, in such cases, we are looking at strong minds who wish to counteract corporate greed and social injustices. What causes envy and covetousness in the first place? Greed. One must have what the other has— that is greed. Greed is closely related to envy. They say that greed is the act of holding onto what is your own, but this is not the case. Greed is the act of taking what belongs to someone else. That is greed. So as you can very clearly see, greed can be present in the hearts of rich and poor alike. The poor man may very possibly be far more greedy than the rich man, because whilst he has little, he wishes to take what the other has. And the rich man may very well be more generous than the poor man, because whilst he has a lot and he creates more for himself and his family, he is also happy to help others as much as he can and he might not wish harm to anyone else, not even to those who have more than he has. Of course, there are the generous amongst the poor, as well. There are also the greedy amongst the rich. But I am saying that the uprightness of a man's heart cannot be measured by the presence or the absence of money.

Gradually, the desire to have what another has, becomes the desire to have *more* than what the other has and this is called 'insatiable greed'. Those who seek to counteract insatiable greed are not evil in nature. This is not the type of 'equality' that I am referring to.

The type of equality that I am referring to, is the type that is born from greed. And greed has many faces. Simple faces, kind faces, undressed faces, lowly faces— hiding inside lowly hearts can be found the most venemous forms of evil. This is why I say, that there are poor men who are evil and rich men who are evil. There are poor men who are good and rich men who are good. We cannot see this on the outer face of man; one must have eyes to see the inner face of man in order to see these things.

To counteract greed and to counteract insatiable greed, is to remain divergent. It is very difficult for the divergent to stay truly divergent, since the currents are strong currents and are often deceptive. To remain divergent, you must remove yourself from unnecessary passion. It is not passion that should drive your cause because it is that same passion that is so easily corrupted. When passion is met by passion, this is not oil and water! But when passion is met by passion, no matter if it is mutual or opposing in nature, this is like wine meeting wine. Two wines can still mix, though they come from different bottles! And this is easily had.

To stay your course on the battlefield, to remain divergent— remove yourself from passions. Do what you do only because it is the right thing to do, not because your heart burns with a passion for it, not because your heart is ablaze.

You may use your Fire, either way, you see. A fire may be used to neutralise: in this case, burn your passion away, do not identify it with the Flame. A fire may also be used to promulgate: in this case, you would be defining your passion as the Flame itself, and calling it as such.

To remain divergent, to remain neutral, you must use your Fire to neutralise, to burn away what should not be there."

"Is this not the same nature shared by water? That water washes away? We all know that water washes away what we do not want to have around us or on us. So in this sense, Water is sharing the nature of Fire as you have explained to me and since this is the case, that means they are functioning the same way!"

"That is not so. Indeed, water washes away and removes what we do not want to have around us or on us. But observe how it does this. In order to wash away, it must remove itself from itself, losing a significant part of it in the process. Water must move away and detach from initial source in order to wash away. In doing this, it has also removed from itself and diminished itself. So, it is not only the thing removed that has been removed; but it is also the water itself that is depleted. This is very different.

If you identify as Water and move and breathe as Water does, you will lose big parts of yourself during the removal of those things that should not be a part of you. In the washing you will also be depleted, just as water is— so will you be too. To remove, you will also remove from yourself! Even just to move, you will have to thin yourself out, changing your structure. The less you move, the stronger you are; but the more you move, the less powerful you become. Rivers always move, they are far less powerful than the ocean. When the ocean moves, it does not really go anywhere; rather, it simply roars, raises, crashes and falls. All of this behaviour of water is almost the complete opposite behaviour compared to fire, compared to flame!

Fire moves as one, not extinguishing or removing from itself in any way and when it is time to remove something from itself, it becomes stronger in the process. When you are of the Fire, of the

Flame, you do not remove from yourself in order to remove anything from you; moreover, you do not move away from yourself! Fire must always be One in order to exist! Parts of it may not be removed from it. Remember this. It moves as One. When you are Flame, you move into and about all things as One– never removing yourself from yourself, but instead, you grow stronger in every movement that you make! A moving Fire is the stronger Fire; unlike moving Water. Fire moves and grows in and of itself, both at the same time. If you are Fire, you may remove things from yourself without depleting from yourself; even better, you may remove things from yourself while growing stronger, more powerful. As Fire, you may burn away things and grow stronger all at once. Water cannot do this. And so as you can now see, the nature of Water and Fire are not identical, they do not have the same capacities.

When I was of the Water, I would either harden in the presence of negative energy, or I would deplete myself by attempting to wash it away. In other cases, the objects of negativity would sink into my depths and actually become a part of me. All of these scenarios were harmful to my Soul, Mind, Heart, Body. These are all situations that will not ever happen to one who is of the Fire. Nothing may sink into Fire and become a part of it; nothing may be removed by Fire and remove *from* Fire at the same time; Fire will never harden in the presence of what it wishes to shun.

Why does Water have these reactions? It is simple. When Water wishes to shun an energy, or an object, the best way to do this is by freezing. Becoming frozen will not allow these objects and these energies to sink into it and at the same time, freezing is an action that will ensure protection from depletion! In order to protect itself, Water will freeze, because if not, it will either lose itself or it will take into itself that which should not be there (or that which it does not understand or does not want). But becoming frozen alters the state of the Water and affects everything around it, not just those objects that it wishes to have an effect upon. It is true that perhaps you could say, that Fire also has an effect on everything it touches, even those things that it does not wish to touch; but it remains a fact that Fire does not need to protect itself because it is rather others that must protect themselves from it. If Fire perchance touches that which it does not wish to touch, that is of no harm to itself, because the chemical structure of it is not altered. It will not need to 'unfreeze' itself later on in order to return to Love, to Innocence, to Warmth, to Friendship. It never loses its original structure, through all times."

"I am now feeling a little perplexed... which is better to be? Of the Fire or of the Water?"

"Like I have already told you, if you are of the Fire, then it will be better for you to move and flow in the characteristics of Fire. And if you are of the Water, then it will be better for you to move and to flow with the characteristics of Water. We are not all the same, you see."

"Can we teach others to be of the Fire? And how is it that you were once of Water and now of Fire?"

"I liked Water! But it was never good for me. The freezing, the hardening, the washing away… it all went against my nature and there was a constant struggle within me. And when I say constant struggle, I mean a palpable, ongoing and relentless inner motion of struggle. Because my nature was the opposite of Water. My nature was always of Fire.

What we can do is teach the ways of the Fire to those of the Fire. They will know it is they by the song that they answer to, they will come. They will come when they hear. If they are not of Fire, then they will not hear and they will not come. I can teach the Philosophy of Fire to those of the Fire, they will understand and they will comprehend. I don't have to teach this to all people, though. Not all people are of my concern."

"Are Fire Beings of the Sun or of the Moon? It seems like an obvious answer, but it is not! Fire is of the Sun, but it is the darkness that needs the Light!

Fire is Light. Darkness is ruled by Selene, by Moon! So this makes me wonder and this makes me ask, is Fire of Moon or of Sun?"

"To answer this, let me tell you a story. When you listen to my story, you will understand it and you will see the answer to your question.

There are children of the Moon and there are children of the Sun. The Moon children think deeply, contemplate often, they ponder upon things like 'meanings' and 'sources'. They move with a collective inner motion, like the tides that are bound to the Moon. The Sun children frolick often; will invite you to play with them; their hair is burnt and so is their skin. Their smiles contagious as a disease yet harmless as honey. And then there are some who are half Moon and half Sun; like the cycles of day and night, there is a setting Sun and a rising Moon within them. There is a noontime and a midnight. They are both pensive and playful; they are both deep and shallow. They can rise a Moon within them when they wish to and rise a Sun within them when they want to. You can find them in the mountains, halfway between the sea and the sky. There they dance around bonfires and gaze into the flames they have lit."

"This means that to be of the Fire is to be of both the Moon and the Sun!"

"You have understood well."

"What shall we call the ones who are of Fire? Should we say, 'Fire Beings' or should we say 'Children of the Fire' or should we say, 'Salamanders' after the elementals of the Flames? What should we call ourselves?"

"Anybody of the Fire may call themselves anything that they wish. Long ago, they called themselves Fire Philosophers. The Keepers of the Flame. As for me, I call myself a Dragon. Not because I am a reptile, but because the treasure of Dragons is the Flame. And because the Dragon Creed of olde is also my Creed. Long before I discovered the Dragon Creed, I lived by it. I knew it by heart. When I finally heard it one day, I was simply hearing what I already knew by heart and then I thought and said to myself, 'this is my Creed.' Therefore, I call myself a Dragon. I know that many call themselves this, but, there may be many that are of the same surname but not of the same blood. It is not necessarily the case that all of the same surname also share the same blood. Many are labelled as diamonds but only a few diamonds are worth millions. Not all are the same. You may call those of the Fire— Dragons. But they may choose to call themselves differently. And many call themselves Dragons, but they share no semblance to or with me."

"Does it make sense to say that the Keepers of the Flame are Dragons, because it is the Dragon who treasures the Fire?"

"Yes, it does make sense to say this."

"Are you not afraid of Dragons? Are they not very frightening, powerful beings?"

"I would have been afraid of Dragons, if I did not slowly come to the knowledge that I was raised by them, protected by them, taught and guided by them. Dragons watch over me. They shapeshift. I thought I was guarded by a Tiger, but later I learned that my Tiger was a Dragon in Tiger form. I was not afraid of my Tiger, so why should I be afraid of my Tiger's original form?

There is nothing more powerful than the Dragon, so yes, they are powerful and it would be wise to fear them. But I am of them, therefore, I do not fear them. How can I fear what is my own?"

"Could we call the Children of the Moon and the Sun— Dragons?"

"We could if we wanted to, yes. I am not here to tell anybody what to call things. I may guide you unto a flower and give the flower to you, but if you want to call that flower a rose even if others would call it a peony, this does not affect the flower itself.

And it does not affect you, either. Therefore, call the flower what you wish to call the flower. I know what to teach you and I know what to teach them. That includes knowing what I do not need to teach you and knowing what I do not need to teach them. I do not need to teach anyone what to call the flowers. I need only to show them where the flowers are and maybe even pick the flowers and place them into their hands. I can give you the names, but those names do not need to be the final outcome."

"What can you say, though, about the fact that fire may be extinguished by water? Everyone knows this."

"Indeed, fire may be extinguished by water. And a small fire may be extinguished by wind. Fire may also be eliminated by earth. Why, is it a competition to see who is more powerful? It is not.

In Fire, we may find both absolute Power and absolute Humility. There is no element more powerful, and yet, there is no element that is more easily extinguished by another. But it is not extinguished, you see. It gives way, but, it always lights itself somewhere else. If a Flame is gone from here, you can be sure it has ignited somewhere else. If a Flame is gone from there, you can be sure it may ignite itself somewhere here. An ocean may be dried up completely by the Sun and that would be the end of it. It is not so with Fire. A mountain may be flattened, and that is the end of it. You may argue that a mountain rises somewhere else; but, it is not the same mountain. Fire is always the same Fire. Have you noticed this? Have you noticed that Fire is always the same Fire? Fire does not change; it only grows or goes away. You might say that water always returns as itself, as well. But the mere fact that it is reprocessed by the Sun means that it is altered. There is also the fact that it freezes and changes its nature entirely, in its frozen state. Water is so affected by the temperature of air that it freezes and so affected by the temperature of fire that it melts. The temperature of fire also affects the air and also the Earth.

All the elements affect all the other elements, yet none are the same. It is like human beings. We must accept that we are not all the same, and yet we may affect one another. Fire is able to affect the other elements to a great deal, all without altering itself nor removing from itself. And yet, it may easily give way to water, to air, to earth. Powerful and Humble. But Humility *is* Power, anyway."

"This reminds me of the Yin and Yang principles that you discussed with me earlier. Is the Yin and Yang in fact repeated throughout all of nature? Is this in fact a fundamental particle of life and of nature?"

"I do believe so. To understand the Yin and Yang, is to understand all of Life and all of Nature. The most relatable and immediate and beautiful example that I can give you right now, is the example of the man and the woman.

They will tell you that you need no one, they will tell you that you must be fully whole on your own, that nobody else is able to fill you up, that nobody else is your 'other half'. You must be a whole all on your own, because there is no other person who may make you whole, due to the fact that there is no other person who is your other half. That is what they have told you and that is what they will continue to tell you. And yet, look at the person who tells you this. That person, just like every other person on this planet, is two halves of two different people! Every whole is comprised of two halves of separate people! It is a primeval, primordial, scientific and undeniable fact, that each human being on this planet (and each human being who has ever existed in history) has come about as a result of two different human beings coming together. Each person is two halves of two other people. You in your wholeness came into existence because of two people that happened to become your parents. You are two halves that make one different whole. And all the other human beings whom you will bring into this world, are going to be a half of you and a half of someone else (if you reproduce biologically with your own body).

You cannot tell two halves that they are one whole, by removing the fact that to create anything whole, two are needed! Insanity of all insanities! And yet, you are being taught an insanity! And they are being taught an insanity. We are all being taught an insane teaching!

The truth is that these teachings arise from the need to fill in gaps that have been created by losses. These are the things that people want others to believe and that they themselves want to believe, after the fact that they have lost so much. Our most early losses in life are usually caused by the breaking apart of two people: our parents. We usually heal, later on, only to repeat the same brokenness in our own relationship/s later on in life. We shatter again. Then we lie to ourselves and tell ourselves that we need no one. And other people lie to themselves and tell themselves the same thing. What is the fact of life, though? The fact of life is that you wanted your parents to stay together, because they created you. You lost that when they broke apart. You probably lost that again repeatedly in your own life, repeating the sorrow for your own children.

Your most important relationship in life is your relationship with your significant other. In this relationship, you should create a space where there is no room for competition, no room for manipulation, no room for comparisons, arrogance, envy, treachery or betrayal. That person needs to be— and should be— the other half of you, the one who stands beside you, the other half of you, the one who is on your side. You need to have that space in this world that you create with that person, a space which you safeguard with your very life. Because it *is* life.

Your significant other is the core of your family. Without the other, your children would not exist. Your relationship with your children is not your primary relationship in life; nor is the relationship you have with your parents. Look at it this way: Your relationship with your parents exists because they are two people who came together. Your relationship with your children exists because you came together with someone else. How much happier and better off would you be, if the relationship between your parents thrived? And how much happier and better off would your children be if your relationship with your significant other thrived/ thrives? All of the other relationships are branches stemming from one main and most important relationship. The fundamental particle.

What is the fundamental particle? Yin and Yang. What is Yin and Yang? Female and Male. Darkness and Light. Water and Fire. Earth and Heaven. This is not to say that these elements or states of existence are particularly exclusive either to the male or to the female; rather, this is to say that there is unity in opposites. Regardless of which sex those opposites may be thriving in/ as a part of.

Not all human beings are going to find their other half the first time. Life changes, paths deviate, and sometimes we meet others before we meet our other half. If it is truly your other half that you want to find in this lifetime, then you will not stay with any of the others. This is just the way that it is. It has been written that in the coming together of the two halves of a whole, there is much joy but also much sorrow. It has been written that this process strikes sorrow into the heart of God— because oftentimes, in the coming together of the original whole, relationships must be torn apart. Though there is joy in the reconstruction of an original existence; there is also sorrow in the demolition of existing relationships in order to recreate the original form. In layman's terms: many marriages may be demolished because the true desire of your Soul is to be reunited with your other half in this lifetime. That is both a great triumph and a deep sorrow. But then again, seldom are great triumphs born without deep sorrows.

When you *do* reunite with your other half, safeguard that union in a space of safety. Do not allow the negative undercurrents of envy, comparisons, competition, treachery, manipulation and distrust to carry you underwater. This relationship must be your primary concern in life. It must be the core from which all of the others flow. It must be untainted by the lies that you hear from the media, from jealous people, from mainstream thought. This union must be the union of two who are always on each others' side. It must be your Life. Because it *is* your Life. It is the root of Life, in everyone's lives!"

"If this is Life, then why do we all end up so afraid of having it? Do we not all fundamentally long for Life? Then why do we run away from exactly what we long for, at the end of the day?"

"Why are we all so afraid of this? That is easy. To lose this would mean to lose your Life. You may still stand breathing, but, to breathe does not mean to be alive! To be alive is something else on the inside. So, along with this truth comes a big fear of loss. If it hurts to lose what is lesser— how much more to lose what is so much greater! But then ask yourself this— maybe the lesser is lost for the sake of the greater, why shouldn't that be the case? Maybe what is eternal, remains eternal! Maybe marriages don't work out, because though we have promised someone the rest of our lives, meanwhile, we may very well have promised someone else the rest of eternity, many lifetimes ago! It could very well be, that the reason why many marriages and relationships fail, is due to the fact that promises are never really broken. We may have promised someone else something so much bigger and better, many lifetimes ago. Perchance at the beginning of all time!"

"What is the Creed of the Dragons? I want to learn it, I want it to be my Creed, too."

"I will gladly teach you the Creed of Dragons. There was a Creed written a very long time ago, which you may find on your own. But I will teach you my own Creed of Dragons, which I have learned to put into practice.

Firstly, let all that you do never be for fame or for recognition in a world filled with people that do not care about you. Even if they do care about you, do nothing for fame and for their recognition. But all that you do should be done to know and to be known by the few people around you whom you Love and who Love you. To know and to be known means to Love. To fall into a life shared together. There are a few people in your life who are worthy of that. We live for those whom we call our family; not for the world and all the rest of its inhabitants; not for superficial charm, not for fame. We live to Love and to be Loved. To live a Life worthwhile is to live a Life of family.

Secondly, may all of your actions benefit you and those whom you Love and who Love you. May your deeds be beneficial first and foremost to your family and to yourself. Think first of your family and of their happiness. It is good to think of the wellbeing of the planet and of the rest of the people in it, but, this must be an afterthought. A Dragon already knows that what will benefit his family, are actions that will ultimately also benefit everyone else. But he does these actions with Love in his mind: with family in his mind. The rest may benefit from the overflow.

They say that greed comes from thinking of one's own interests, but to a Dragon, this is not so. The right things are right through and through and what is right through and through is beneficial to all of humankind. To do right by your family will cause more right to be done in the world, by others. Therefore, our greatest good that is done, is done to our family, to those whom we Love and who Love us.

The greatest shame in a Dragon's eyes is to be unable to effectively Love his or her family, those who have been given him/her to Love. This is a shame that the Dragon must avoid at all costs. Your other half comes first; together the two of you shall Love your family; then your family as a whole shall love its friends; then your family and friends together shall love your nation; then your nation, after loving her own people, shall share this love with other nations. This is the only way. In all things, I always say that there are many ways, but in this thing, I will tell you the truth— that there is only this one way.

Love the other half of your Soul in such a way that if you were the only person left on the face of the Earth, you would still look into the mirror and say that you have Loved your other half through and through. Not for the eyes of men, but as an attribute of your own Soul. Be loyal, be faithful, be trustworthy to the One whom you Love. Everything else is weakness, is bondage, is slavery to the ailments that afflict the aging flesh of the human. Take part in nothing else but what is faithful, loyal and trustworthy within your own Mind and within your own Soul.

The Third tenet to know, is that, to dishonour another is to dishonour oneself. If you dishonour someone through the betrayal of trust or through humiliation or any other means of dishonouring another person, you must know that you have also dishonoured yourself. To wound another is to wound yourself. Unless the other has done you serious harm to Soul or to Body, do not dishonour him or her. What you have done to another, you have done also to yourself. Not because you are one flesh and one heart with everyone, but simply because as you wrongfully and willingly harm another one, you are returning pain unto yourself.

The Fourth tenet to know, is that, Dragons are to be bound to Honour and free from slavery. Bind yourself to your Honour, to your Nobility, to your Creed; and free yourself from slavery by freeing yourself from the temporary state of feelings that come and go. They who are not Dragons follow whatever feeling that comes their way! And they define this as freedom! This is the opposite of the Dragon; for he who is Dragon, is not swayed by feeling, for he knows that emotions are temporary. Creed and Honour are Final. And Creed and Honour may never be an act done for the eyes of others, for this cancels out the First and Second tenets of the Creed. Even if you were to be the only person left living on this planet, you would still follow your Creed, you would still hold on to your Honour, though there be no eyes to see it— because you are

Dragon. You hold onto your Honour because you will always have to live with *you*, for as long as you exist, you will be existing with *you*. Do you want to exist alongside and within a fraud, a fake, a fallacy? Or do you want to Live within and alongside the Nobility, the Honourable, the Worthy? It is *you* who determines this.

We hold steadfast to our Creed not because others may see what we are doing; but because *we* can see what we are doing! We do not follow whims of the emotions; we hold fast unswayed by these. We remain loyal, strong, worthy enough to trust our own selves. The Nature of the Flame is the Nature of the Dragon. We Trust ourselves more than anyone else; not because others are not trustworthy, but because we have gained our own Trust first! We have gained the Trust of ourselves. I Trust me first, and I will Trust other Dragons, too, for I know they share in my Creed.

To be a slave is to come and go at every whim of one's emotions! This is slavery. To have no control over one's sexual impulses is to be slave to one's mortal flesh. To have no control over the things that tempt our flesh is to be slave to anything and anyone that tempts us. Those who are not of the Fire call that freedom! In reality, they are slaves! And one day they will die as slaves!

The Fifth tenet that you must know, is that Lightness of Being, Happiness and Joy are treasures that are found both in the child and in the one dedicated to Creed. They will tell you that to have Honour, Nobility, Responsibility and Loyalty are traits that may not coincide with Happiness, Lightness and Joy. They will tell you that you must become slave to flesh in order to find these treasures. This is, of course, untrue. One may be responsible and Happy. One may be loyal and Joyous. One may be dedicated and at the same time carry an incredible Lightness of Being. This is the state of the Dragon. These sought-after treasures do not follow those who are slaves to the flesh; they are abundant for those who are bound to Honour.

The Sixth tenet you must know,is that, what is yours must remain as yours. Protect what is your own. Do not remove from yourself to give unto others. Remember the Flame. If you do give unto others, may it be because they have gathered around your Flame and are warmed by your Fire; may it never be because you have taken what belongs to your family, what belongs to your spouse, what belongs to those whom you Love and who Love you, in order to give unto others. Do not allow hair-thin cracks to fester in between the relationships that are the most important to you; because where there is a crack, there will always be another person from the outside who will want to fit into it. Make no room for such destructions. Fortify your family— your family is yours. Fortify your most important relationship— your partner/spouse is yours. As you are your own, he or she is your own. Not as an object, but as your own flesh. Dragon unto Dragon; Creed unto Creed. As the Dragon guards its Treasures, you guard your Treasures also. As the

Dragon allows in only the Pure of Heart, you also allow in only those Pure of Heart.

Then fight to protect what is yours and to keep what is yours. Dragons belong only to those who can and who will fight for them; likewise, a Dragon will always put up a fight for those he or she Loves and for what he or she Loves.

The Seventh tenet that you must practice, is that you must waste none of your moments and none of your time on those who do not have Creed. Dragon unto Dragon; Creed unto Creed. If there are those who do not share your Creed, waste no time with them, unless they seek to learn your Creed and they seek it with sincerity of heart. Then you may take your time with them. Teach another Dragon if you find another Dragon. But waste not your time with those who are unlike you.

The Eighth tenet to live by, is to not be easily angered. To be easily angered is to be a slave to one's emotions. Do not be easily hardened like water, but learn to dance up and down, learn how to twist and reach and bow— all like the Flame. Remember always that the Flame knows how to bow and how to rise, to dance here and to dance there— it does not change, it only sees how to give way. It is humble, it is flexible, it always remains soft. Like the Flame, learn to be soft and to bow when needed. Be not led so quickly to anger.

The Ninth tenet to live by, is to stand by those Pure in Heart. Purity of heart can be found amongst the rich and the poor alike, a Dragon knows purity not by classification of social standing, but by the eyes with which to immediately see the Heart. They will tell you that all who are poor are Pure and that all who are rich are impure— this is an outright lie! There are as many evil amongst the poor as there are amongst the rich. Look into the Hearts, with no regard to social standing. You may share your treasures with the Pure in Heart, but do not share your treasures with those who do not know how to remember a good deed done unto them.

The Tenth tenet to put into practice, is that we must always repay kindness with kindness. But do not stop there. Continue to repay kindness done unto you with kindness in return. Do not think that once is enough. Plant that seed given to you, plant it into fertile ground, then water the flower that grows, watering with loving actions and with kind, thoughtful deeds. May no one regret showing you kindness; but on the contrary, may they consider it amongst their greatest investments in life! Do not repay a person for their goodness only once; rather, be the gardener of their goodness and continue to water and to admire the flower that grows from that seed.

On the other hand, if someone is not capable of repaying your kind actions with equal acts of kindness in return, forget about that person, remove your affections for them. To forget lovingkindness done unto you and to not help those who have helped you in the past, is the lowest state of the human being. Do not associate with those of such a low state.

The Eleventh tenet to live, is to never abandon the one you Love during times of hardship. The harder the path, the stronger your grip; the more difficult the times, the more fervent your Love; the colder the winds, the closer you hold onto one another. There is only shame to be found in the eyes of the one who abandons the one he loves in times of hardship. First and foremost this is applicable to family (which is spearheaded by your other half); secondly, it is applicable to friends. Do not trust anyone who would use a time of hardship to gain a foothold above you, do not trust anyone who would use a time of difficulty to gain a one up over another. Do not trust the weak— those who change when the winds blow cold.

The Twelfth tenet to live, is to know that your word is your bond. The word of a Dragon is written upon a mountain, carved into the stone, then set ablaze with fire. *That* is how much of a bond your word should be. Your word is powerful not only in the speaking but also in the keeping. You must know that when you say you will do something, your word is bound to the chemical makeup of your body. We are unlike those of this world, whose word cannot be trusted. We do what we say we will do, because when we speak it, we have bound our bodies to keep it. Therefore, give not your word lightly and give not your word to those who are unlike you, for to be taken advantage of is a very painful experience.

The Thirteenth tenet to live, is to never be afraid to stand alone. This is a very important one. A Dragon is never afraid to stand alone. Do not care if your thoughts on matters are wholly unlike everyone else's thoughts on matters, do not feel ashamed if your opinion on an event or a circumstance is a the opposite of everybody else's opinion of it. In fact, what a bondage it is to live in a herd, bound to what the rest of the herd does, thinks, feels! That is one of the greatest bondages that the humans experience in life, that they do not feel confidence, they do not feel freedom, they do not feel courageous unless there are a million others by their side.

You may stand there with a million at your side and still be wrong. I may stand here, all alone, only me, but still be right! Numbers do not produce uprightness, courage, intelligence, or truth! Do not be afraid— listen to me, never be afraid— to hold an opinion wholly different from your friends, your peers, the rest of the world. They will attempt to make you feel like an outcast, they will attempt to make themselves look like the better ones, but you are Dragon and no Dragon is afraid to fly or to stand alone. Believe what you know in your heart to be True, believe what you know in your heart to be courageous, believe what you know in your heart to be upright. Stand alone, stand strong. Know that when you stand in Uprightness, Courage and Truth, the Gods stand with you. Even if no other man stands with you, every God stands with you. In the knowledge of this take courage. Remember that we see the fruit before the tree has bore it! This means that there will be many times when your persuasion of what is upright and just, is entirely against what everyone else believes to be upright and just. They base their decisions upon the tree; while you base your decisions upon the fruit! In the knowledge of this, take courage. Though you stand alone, you never really *are* alone!"

"I am curious to know if it is truly harmless to be okay with standing alone. After all, we should all just accept the fact that we are needy and needful of one another/ of others. To be okay with standing and flying alone might produce a loneliness and a type of character that denies neediness in any form."

"Indeed, it is easy to get too wrapped up in the thirteenth tenet, that you begin to shut out those whom you *do* need, whom you *do* want and whose opinions truly matter to you. It is an undeniable fact that we *do* need to care about our differences between others, especially those certain others whose presence are hugely and genuinely meaningful to our lives. It indeed becomes too easy to give the cold shoulder to those whom we truly care about, due to the thirteenth tenet.

It will therefore be extremely beneficial for you to remember that there will be those who are worthy to stand by you and you are in turn also worthy to stand by them— let them in! Do not choose to fly or to stand alone when you no longer need to fly alone, when you no longer need to stand alone. *Do not shut the right people out.* Also, please remember always, that many times it is more important to nourish a relationship than to be right.

The key is to be able to distinguish between the relationships that should be nourished above and more importantly, than your uprightness. This takes us back to the prior tenets, the ones that reinforce the absolute importance of valuing those whom you Love and who Love you. This takes us back to the importance of knowing that not all are of the same value and not all should be of the same value in your heart and in your mind. Some relationships are so important, that it is better to nourish them than to choose to stand alone in your uprightness. Be vigilant and discriminative enough to know which relationships hold this much value in your heart, mind, life. Then, by all means, choose *not* to stand alone! Choose the person over being right. Being right, after all, is *nothing* compared to being in Love!"

"I want to talk to you about the state of the world that we live in right now. How am I to place meaning, how am I to understand? How am I to know, how am I to navigate? In the Creed of the Dragons, you have mentioned people being the same and not being the same (Dragon unto Dragon, Creed unto Creed). I wish to understand this further, in an expanded way, I want to understand the expanse of this belief and I want to understand more precisely the issues of inequality. I am taught always that inequality is the great Daemon of this Earth, eating away at the carcasses of man. I am taught daily to see and to expect my brother and my sister to be just as myself— for we are one. If this is true, then why do things not change? The more we believe this, the more we fall! I want to rise as the Dragons rise, so teach me. Tell me, show me. Show me more!"

"I will gladly teach you, my love. Listen to me closely, for what I believe is what you believe. For you and I are one. I believe that even though we believe very strongly in a creed, religion, spirituality or the like; we still need to have a sense of responsibility for our physical, corporeal existence. Time and time again, humanity goes out of balance and leans to one side of the pendulum entirely. We are incorporeal as a Soul, but, we are corporeal as a physical Body, as well. Remember this: that a Body without a Soul is dead. But that a Soul without a Body is without Destiny. Destiny is given unto Souls within Bodies, Destiny is rolled up within lives on this Earth to unravel and to carry out. I am a firm believer in the fact that Body and Soul are of equal importance. The fact that one is temporal and the other is not, does not make the temporal one any less important. Without your temporal Body, your Soul would cease to interact with the living on this corporeal plane. It is a *Gift* and a *privilege* to be able to interact with the living in this corporeal realm. It is a Gift to have some people who love you and whom you love. It is a Gift to touch another's skin and to hold another in one's arms. It is a Gift to experience what being human is like.

Life is difficult and we often feel shorthanded in life by the actions of others towards us. But this does not remove from the Gift. In this world, nothing is equal. To create everything as equal would be to create a uniform civilisation. There is not Beauty in this. Many are wronged and many are shorthanded, but the value of the *Gift* is not measured by who has more or who has better! All who are alive, are equal in the fact that they are alive. All other reasons to hate life are brought about by the belief that all persons and all beings and all people must be equal, must be the same. We are not the same. And other people are allowed to be different from us. And many will have more than what you have in life, but it is the Gift of Life that is greater than all of those material things. The Gift of Life is greater! Death is not a gift. Death is the ending of a life on Earth— how are you going to live your short, short life?

Though we have our religions, our creeds, our spiritual beliefs— these do not supersede nor exceed the importance and the value of our physical Bodies, or of our physical lives here on this Earth. We are not primarily *what* we *believe*. We are primarily *what* we *are!*

People think the problem is that we are not all equal. But I believe the problem is that we expect everyone to be the same and we are shocked when there's something different. We call these differences 'inequalities'. A person who goes about in life being told that everyone and everything are supposed to be 'equal', will inevitably become bitter and resentful at the discovery that his expectations will *never* become reality. When you are a millionaire, there will still be billionaires. When you are a billionaire, there will still be those who are billionaires too, but are happier than you are. When you believe in your God, there will always be others who believe in a different God. And their Gods might teach them differently from your God. We will never be the same and we cannot go about in the world expecting that. It is unrealistic and it sets everyone up for frustration.

Moreover, too many become too enchanted with the spiritual aspect of their existence, they neglect the physical, seeing death as a gift rather than life itself as a gift! This happens to all spiritualities and all religions! The loss of enchantment with physical life does not equate to a highly evolved, spiritual person. But I believe that the loss of enchantment with physical life is a result of the deterioration of balance. The goal must not be to rot the physical away, the goal must be to develop all aspects of man in balance— equally! The equality that a man seeks on the outside, can only be achieved within his own person. When you develop The Threefold Equality (Mind, Soul, Body), this is the only equality that may be achieved. But when it is achieved within every person, this will lead to peace in this world.

Listen closely, for these you must always remember. In this world, we all have the right to not be the same, to be different from any other person. There is no such thing as all being equal or the same. There *is* such a thing as all being different and being *not* the same. When my right to be different, says that your right to be different is lesser than my own, then there is a problem with the way I believe and I must fix it. Because there is no law in the universe that is greater than the law of Freedom. The law of Freedom is only Freedom when all share the same Freedom to be free! And the only way that we may all share that same Freedom, is if each one of our beliefs *stop* at the beginning of another person's belief. When your right to be different tells you that my kind of different is less important than your own, then you must *stop* yourself and change your beliefs. We must be able to change our beliefs whenever we see that those beliefs are telling us that the way someone is different is a wrong way to be different because we believe it is wrong. Our belief of sin is not the same as that other person's belief of sin. The real sin is when we all begin telling each other that the other one is sinning because it is against our own beliefs. *That* is where the line of our personal freedoms must be drawn. And we must be responsible enough to draw them, ourselves. May our freedoms not require the elimination of another person's rights. Our right to be different only lasts as long as that right says that others may be different, too. And God forbid that we go walking around disillusioned in this world, expecting everyone to be equal and to be the same because this will only cause bitterness and frustration. We meet people who are not the same as us, every single day. We meet people with different Gods, every day! We do not all need to share the same God. We do not all need to believe that we were made by the same God! We only need to know that everyone is allowed to believe and to not believe, as they wish. We must go out into the world expecting to encounter all kinds of different.

The propagated notion that we need to *all* see each other as the same, is the wrong path for humanity. Some of us are family, some of us are lovers, some of us are the same because we are kin, because we choose one another, because we share the same values. Now *that* is a sameness worth protecting! As far as I know, I am the only one who has been saying this, to date. If there are others saying the same thing, I would like to meet them. But today I believe that what we are really seeing in this world is the result of the false path that humanity has long accepted as the one path of truth. The answer is never to try to make all the same in our eyes, not even to make all as equal in our eyes. You think that the problem is the lack of sameness. But the lack of sameness is not a problem because it is nature. The lack of the acceptance of differences is the problem.

Why have we had religions overthrowing other religions, since the beginning of time? This is due to the belief that there is one God for all of mankind, therefore, my God must be your God and how are we to reach that? We can only reach that when I am able to make you worship my own God. We have seen this time and time again, throughout history. We saw it with Christianity overthrowing Paganism and with Islam then later overthrowing Christianity and it goes on and on in a loop that does not end! Why? Due to the belief that we all need to believe that we were all made by one God!

What if I was made by my God and you were made by your God and they over there were made by their God? And what is wrong with that? In reality, if humanity were to cease with the desire to believe that we are all created by the same God, then humanity would, in turn, cease to try and make other people believe in their own God. I say we were created by whoever we believe created us! And if you believe that no one created you, how does that affect my life? Then go ahead and do not believe in what you do not want to believe in! We do not need to be the same! I do not need to see myself in you and you should not need to see yourself in me!

Unity is not the belief that we are all the same. Unity is the acceptance of the fact that we are all different. People do not despise people because they are different. People despise other people because they expect them not to be different. Expect all to be different and the world will find peace!"

"Is it right and is it beneficial to believe that we were all created by the same God?"

"The problem with the belief that we are all created equally, would go back to the notion that we are all created by one God. But then others believe we were all created by THEIR one God. And then even more people— over there— believe we were all created by THEIR one God. And so there is a fight to make all people the same kind of equal as created by the same kind of God. Which puts us right back at the original problem. What I do, is I think of all people created by whatever God they believe in, maybe even created in a different way that their God chose to create them in and that is okay and that would be acceptable and beautiful. In this way, I am able to do two things simultaneously: I am able to fully respect their beliefs while fully realising the differences between their belief and my own (and in doing so, I give the same amount of respect to my own beliefs). Herein equality is created. This is the kind of equality that I believe will bring true peace. I believe this is the actual meaning of equality and that this actual meaning has long been overlooked.

In this present day, everyone who believes in a God is loyal to the notion that all people were made by one God (their God), and if others don't believe it, that would be just because they are lost. But then everyone thinks this. So everyone is in the wrong, in the eyes of everyone else! But what if we were to give such an ample amount of respect to one another, enough to truly honour the beliefs of the other by saying, 'Yes, you were created by your God and I was created by my own, because that is the God that you believe in and this is the God that I believe in.'

The other knows that you fully acknowledge they believe what they believe and what they believe may very well be 100% true and accurate for them. Just as what you believe may very well be 100% true and accurate for you!

Our evidence of God on Earth is in our Faith only. By this alone, we should all see that what you believe in makes up your reality. I cannot give you evidence of my God and you cannot give me evidence of yours. But as my God is real to me, so is your God real to you. And we are real— flesh and bone— we do not need to give each other evidence that the other exists! So why should we quarrel over what we, in fact, cannot see?

They say that all paths lead to one source in the end. But I take this further and I say that all paths may lead to their own sources in the end. What if your heaven is different from my heaven? What if your afterlife is different from my afterlife? Maybe we are not all heading to one single afterlife. Do we all head to one single place here on Earth? No. We all choose differently. There is no evidence in nature pointing to the fact that we will all go to the same place in the afterlife. We might all take off in all directions! That is more in tune with nature.

I may believe fully in your beliefs without adhering myself to it and vice versa. It is like how I believe that there is a nation called Iceland and that this nation exists, but I would rather live in the nation called Italy, while you would rather live in Iceland. Now, this is only an example, I do not dislike Iceland. But to give you a very good example of how to see this, because you must see this.

I know that Iceland exists and I know that you want to live there. I do not believe that your belief is false and I do not believe that Iceland is a myth only real to you in your head. But I want to live in Italy, not Iceland. Italy is real and it is where I wish to dwell. Iceland is also real and it is where you wish to dwell. We do not need to bring one another to our dwelling places if the other does not want to go there, but we may at the same time acknowledge that each others' dwelling places do exist and do constitute our realities."

"There is so much darkness in the world and while talking with you, I can see how many various and immense ways all people have been led astray into beliefs that later impact society as a whole, in an evil way. Or at the very least, in a negative way.

I feel lost, I feel afraid, everything is dark all around me and the people hurt each other and there is so much pain, so much loss, so much suffering in this world... help me to understand this, help me to fight it."

"I have been trained in fear combat. And what I mean by that, is I have been trained to fight. I call it fear combat because on the battleground I was able to observe fear at an extremely close proximity. This has been my training for decades, night after night, in my dreams!

There have been times that I have battled entities of pure, unadulterated evil. The feeling of pure evil is identified by the energy that desires to paralyse another. I have stood in front of Satan, himself. Or if you do not wish to call him Satan, you may call him anything else that you wish. But to keep this simple, I have stood in front of Satan, himself. A boy with soft features and a genteel movement of his body. I say 'boy', because he has always been in boy form when I have stood in front of him.

I have stood in front of mere entities without fixed shape. You could call them monsters. There is one whose evil energy is so intense that the air is filled with it, as air is filled with humidity on humid days! Evil like the condensation on the glass of a jar! I had a one-on-one battle with it, within an arena.

I have been able to repeatedly observe fear at these very close proximities. There are two instances in particular, which I will speak to you of in detail so that I may teach you about the enemy and teach you how to overcome it.

I was physically attacked by two different dogs, at two different times. But those attacks did not happen before I had months of training on how to overcome dog attacks. Before I was attacked the first time, I was dreaming for months of a dog attacking me. I dreamt many dreams of the same nature, for many months.

In my dream, the dog snarled and growled and showed its teeth. The look in its eyes would darken and the gaze of insanity would cover them. When the dog would lunge towards me, I would grab the side of its face and squeeze it with all of my might, leaving it inches in front of me, teeth and all, while it screamed in pain!

Over and over again, I was being trained to look and see that the goal of the dog is to intimidate. It shows teeth, growls and becomes filled with an almost paralyzing energy that causes fear to strike at the heart. But listen here: it is still just a dog! The difference takes place when it is able to show you its weapons and in the process of doing that, intimidate you into feeling that it has the power and you are the one without the power. But that is not a fact. The fact is that there is no power removed or taken from you, at all! When you are able to strip the dog of the fear that it attaches itself to, then you are able to see this one simple fact: if you grab its face and squeeze really hard, it doesn't matter if it has twelve rows of razor sharp teeth in its mouth, because that mouth is not going to be able to bite into you! You don't even need to move, you can just stand there, in the exact same position: simply reach out your arm swiftly, squeeze the side of the dog's face with all of your strength and watch it cry.

I did exactly that in my dreams at night— night after night— until only about a second of fear existed between the moment the dog would try to intimidate me and the moment I would squeeze its face with all of my might. That second consists merely of identifying that the fear is present, that's all.

Identify that the fear is being presented to you in order to paralyse you and then immediately strip the object of that fear! When you are able to do this, you are able to see the object for what it is and you will be able to see all of its weak spots. Remember that the goal of fear is always to make you believe that you are powerless. The moment that it strikes, believe that you are in fact powerful! Nothing is taken from you. You do not need to resort to fear mongering in order to overcome another and in that fact alone, you should see that you are the one with true power. You do not need to make yourself bigger and scarier than you are, unlike the object that is harnessing fear in order to try to overcome you. Simply reach out your hand and squeeze the weak spot with all of your might. *There is always a weak spot and you will spot it in the moment that you are able to look past the teeth.*

After I dreamt of the dog attack for months, it happened in my physical reality. And it was a dog who was my friend, the dog belonging to my uncle and his family. Usually, I would pet him and stroke his fur and talk to him. On that particular day, however, he decided to bite me in return! Nothing was out of the ordinary except for his sudden, unexpected actions. I saw the look in his eyes change (that wash of insanity saturating his eyes), then he began to growl, he began to show me his teeth. It took but a second for me to identify the fear and then to go for the weak spots. I hit him hard in the head, and then grabbed onto his face and squeezed with all of my might! He began crying and wiggling, trying to get away from me. Then I let him go and he ran away.

After that first incident, I began to dream again! I dreamt again for about two to four months, the same dream, the same training, the same practice. And then the day came. I was playing in my uncle's big yard, along with their dog (but a different dog, a Doberman). Just like the first dog, this Doberman was usually my friend and we usually got along. Just like the first time, there was nothing out of the ordinary about that day and there was nothing unusual happening until the Doberman decided it was going to bite me! I was simply standing there, smiling and talking to it— and then— that look in the eyes! That look of insanity from absolutely nowhere! I grabbed onto its face just like I did with the first dog, until it cried and squirmed and tried to get away.

The very interesting fact about that second incident, is that there were many adults around, who all became paralysed the minute the doberman began his attack on me! The minute it began to growl, it is like all the adults around stopped breathing and couldn't move. I was only ten years old and my father was there, my uncle was there and my uncle's household staff was there (they employed household staff at their home). But noone could move! Ideally, the ones more physically capable of overcoming that doberman should have jumped in to try and protect me— but due to the paralysing nature of fear and intimidation— they couldn't! And remember this: that is due to the fact that it is not size, age, or the measure of physical strength that is responsible for saving you. But it is the recognition of the weak spot/s! The one who does not feel powerless is the one who will save herself. Remember that. The one who does not feel powerless, will be the one who is able to save herself. I was a small ten year-old-girl. There was nothing physcially extraordinary about me, at all. But there, surrounded by all of those capable adults, I was the only one who did not feel powerless (due to my months of training in my dreams at night), and so I was the one who was able to save myself.

My training I pass onto you now. Strip the object of all that it adds to itself to appear more powerful; strip it with your mind. Look at it as it is. If there is a man with a gun, strip the man of his gun in your mind, look at him, he is still a man covered in skin. There will always be a weak spot. *There will always be a weak spot.*

Nevertheless, the greatest good, is not to come out of a tragedy alive an unscathed— though that is a very good thing— but the greatest good, the ultimate good, is to never be in the vicinity of any tragedy, in the first place. Do not seek to fight, but when you must fight in order to protect yourself or your loved ones, do this without fear and without remorse.

The nature of a living thing changes in toto when it is overcome by that look of insanity that soaks and covers its eyes. It is a cloak of some sorts. Disregard its previous state and realise immediately in that moment, that it is a creature which must be overcome. Plain and simple. Do not stop to think, 'this dog is such a good dog, this dog is my friend, what is happening to this dog, this can't be, what is going on, I don't want to hurt it...' within the moments that it takes you to think these things, you may have already been bitten in the neck and bleeding to death.

Yes, I teach you these things, because you must know them. You were born a warrior, do you not know this? All Queens are trained in both battle and in grace! *Wield your sword and wield your silk with equal proficiency.* Only for one second feel the fear, only to identify it. After that one second is over, slay that fear and overcome the aggressor."

"It rings such a beautiful tune in my ear: 'wield your sword and wield your silk with equal proficiency'. I have never thought of it like that before... is this something that a Queen must do always?"

"A Queen must always know when it is the time to wield her sword and when it is the time to wield her silk. Sword is not silk and silk is not sword. The two are not used interchangeably. But one must know how to use both proficiently and with equal impact. I know both grace and warfare, both silk and sword."

"Is it true what they say, that we should never be afraid of anything? That fear is never the answer to anything and that we must avoid it at all costs? Fearing nothing and seeing the best in everything all around us? Some have said that we must ignore fear and those things that cause fear, that we must act as if the causes of fear do not exist. Is this true?"

"You know, I have many dreams filled with rabbits!

"Dreams filled with rabbits? What a funny thing to say, what could you possible mean by that?"

"In my dreams, the rabbits come to me and I care for them. I learn from them what I must teach to you and what I must teach to the people. They tell the rabbits that the key to overcoming fear, is to dream them away, to imagine that they are not there. But I tell the rabbits that the key to overcoming fear, is knowing the fear, identifying the fear, learning how it moves, learning its nature. You will never overcome *anything* by the imagination of it not being there. Because you cannot change what you imagine to not be there, you cannot fight an unseen enemy. The key is not to *not* see; but the key is in fact *to* see! You must always remember that. Your *sight* is what will set you free.

The medicine for fear, these days, is a dose of reality. Because these days the reality is far worse than the disembodiment of the ideal. People today are afraid of the disembodiment of the ideal, because they think the ideal is the reality. A rabbit that does not know it lives in the ground with snakes, is constantly afraid of the sea hawk possibly finding its way to land, to destroy the rabbit's meadowy existence. In the meadow, living in fear of the sea hawk, not knowing the hole in the ground next to its burrow belongs to a snake. I show the rabbit where the snakes are, thus eliminating its hazardous fear. Misplaced fear is hazardous fear. Fear well placed is a skill for survival. Fear well placed is a chance to outwit, outsmart and overcome that very fear. You have to see your enemy, you have to see the fear.

They have taught the rabbit to never feel fear; instead, they have taught the rabbit to dream. Dream of your meadow: you are in your meadow; dream of the sea: the sea is right next to you; dream of the sea hawk: it is your enemy, it lives in the sea and you live in the meadow but if you dream hard enough, it will never pass your meadow. They have not taught the rabbit that the other holes in the ground do not all belong to rabbits, but some belong to snakes! They have not taught the rabbit that the meadow is nestled in between hills, the sea is far away! They have taught the rabbit a dream, and to dream the dream very hard. They have taught the rabbit never to fear, only to dream.

I teach the rabbit to see the holes, some belong to other rabbits, but others belong to snakes. I teach the rabbit that the meadow is nestled between hills, the sea hawk is far away. The nightmare that the rabbit was taught to dream away will never happen, because the meadow is not where the rabbit thinks it is. But the reality that exists around it, is far worse than the nightmare, for it is there and it is real and the rabbit has not been taught to see the snakes. I tell the rabbit not to fear all things, but to fear some things. To fear some things in order to overcome them.

The meadow is still beautiful, the flowers are all around. The reality is still a wondrous one! But the meadow is not beside the sea and in the ground there are many snakes."

"Your dreams of rabbits taught you all of this?"

"I suppose so."

"What is your one powerful message for humanity, today?"

"This is a great question! I will tell you my message for humanity, so that you may take my message and spread it far and wide. It is time for a change that will shake this Earth until the outer crust crumbles and falls off of it; until the only thing left is that which was meant to be.

We have reached a point in time, a needle-point moment in time, where we will either shake this Earth and her civilisation to the core until it falls away and we may build a new Earth; or, we will all fall asleep and every act of violence and terror will become only like bugs walking across our faces while we are fast asleep. You will either stand up or you will fall asleep. Now is the time.

Humanity, listen to me. So many of our opinions, preferences and presumptions about other people and about what the world must most definitely be like, are placed into our minds by our childhood religions. So few of that is from our own experiences of our lives from outside of that religious blanket.

I cannot give you evidence that my God is real and you cannot give me evidence that your God is real. You may laugh at the stories of my God while I laugh at the stories of your God. In reality, both stories are of absolutely equal reliability. They are stories that we believe. And that is it. Your God lives within your Faith of Him or Her. And my God lives within my Faith of Him or Her. This means that our Gods live for us as individuals and within us as individuals.

You are real and I am real. We need no evidence to prove to each other that the other exists. Then why do we quarrel over the Gods that we cannot see? Your God is real because you are real and within your belief your God lives. My God is real because I am real and within me my God lives. We, therefore, need not mock. We, therefore, need not quarrel.

How much of what your Holy Book says, is what your God says? And how much of it is just what you are saying? You may live as you are and as you choose, for as long as your ways do not dictate that the way I am and the way I live are not supposed to be. What your God says is not supposed to be, may be different from what my God is telling me. But when our Gods have something hateful to say about you and about me, that is when our Gods must no longer dictate us.

Have our Gods ever really, really dictated us? Or have we been dictating our Gods all along?

So much of what we think about others are things we do not know. If someone needs to save my life one day, it will not matter what God they believe in! Would you stop to ask if they are Christian, Muslim or Jew? Would you stop to ask first if they are Pagan, Monotheist or Witch? Or would you just let them save your one precious life?

Humanity, listen to me. It is time for this all to end. It is time for a new beginning."

"What is it that you mean when you ask, 'Have our Gods been dictating us? Or have we been dictating our Gods all along?'"

"I will answer your question with another question: Has your God made you in His image, or is it you who have made your God in your image? But I suppose I should change the nature of my question because we both know that for you and for me, we have not created our Gods in our own image. To reconstruct this question, let me put it like this: 'Have the Gods of all human beings created Their followers in Their own Image; or have all the human beings, grouped together, been creating their Gods in their own images?'

If there is One God who created all of humankind in His One Image, then why is it that in all of humankind, people are divided by their images of their own Gods? If God created all of humankind in His One True Image, then why is the image of God held by of all humankind— divided and different? Surely, a child recognizes the voice of his father? Then why do all people recognize different voices of different Fathers (or Mothers)?

The answer is simple! It's either different Gods have made different people in Their Own Image; or, different kinds of people have made different kinds of Gods, after their own image! Which one do you believe in?

Because we cannot, under any circumstance, believe that One God made all of humankind in His One Image; because if that were so, then that would mean that every single religious person is entitled to believe that their God is the one true God and that their path is the one true path set by God. In such a case, there will *never* be peace! And aside from the fact that there would never be peace, there is also the fact that for everyone to think such a way is absolute lunacy. Because you are all thinking the same thing, and yet simultaneously all of you think that the other is wrong. Then that would mean that all are wrong! That would mean that absolutely no one is right! Our position (in the worldview) of either right or wrong, is determined by how we are placed by others: into either right or either wrong! If we all place the other into the wrong, then that means we are all wrong! And if we are all wrong, then that would mean that there is no God at all! Such would be the birthplace of the atheist. On the other hand, perhaps,the atheist is actually the person who is closest to God! He says he does not believe that there is a God because he cannot believe in all of the religions that the other people hold to be true. In his heart, he still hears the voice of his God calling out His name, he recognizes, he longs, he yearns, he cannot accept Holy Books that were half produced by other men... and so he calls himself an atheist. When in fact, perhaps he is the one closer to God than all of the others!"

"Things are simply not as they seem!"

"Indeed!"

"Like the Flame, for instance, I suspect that the Flame is not simply as it appears to be! How many parts are there to one flame? When you look into the flame on your candlestick, how many parts of it are there? Because I have been told that there are two parts or three parts... you have already taught me of the outer part and the inner part... but I feel as though there is more that you have not yet taught me. When *you* look into the flame, how many parts do *you* see?"

"When I look into the flame, I see six parts. I see three sections of the outer part and three sections of the inner part.

First, there is that blueness at the very beginning of the flame, at the bottom of it, from whence it is born. You will notice the blue colour.Then around that blue color is a transparent flame, which is then surrounded by a dense, yellow flame. These are the three inner parts.

Around the outermost inner section of the flame, there is another structure of the flame outlining it, it is a thin outline, less dense than the outermost of the inner, but denser than the transparent part. The middle of the outer flame is a glow which extends widely around the flame, it is the light that emanates and expands all around it. It is circular and golden-yellow. This middle part grows fainter as it moves out into the expanse around the flame, until, after reaching its faintest parts that have become nearly undetectable, it touches the outermost part of the outer flame: a circular 'rainbow' which encases everything. The first hue that I can see in this 'rainbow' is green, then surrounded by red. These colours are very faint, but, they are there.

The flame having six parts is the reason why I believe that the flame is the best representation of two Souls becoming One. And also a good example of duality within one Soul: the Supreme Self and the Human Self; the Goddess and the Girl. The Warrior and the Child. So on and so forth. As such, I believe the flame is the representation of a Soul as an individual person and of two Souls being a part of One Whole. Soul Mates, Twin Flames, so on and so forth... they have their various names for two Souls that are but One.

The concept of 'twin flames' imagines two flames that have become one and herein this concept falls short. Because it is not two flames become one; but in actuality, it is one flame with six parts. Three belonging to one and three belonging to the other.

You see, there are three parts to each person: The Body, the Mind and the Soul. Each of the three parts of the flame represents each of the three parts of the individual person. Three plus three equals six. Here, six is equivalent to one. Six equals One. Six is One. Therefore, six is the number of wholeness. Wholeness of Love, wholeness of Person reunited with their Other Half. In one flame, we see two halves of a single soul. In one Flame, we see two Souls that are but One."

"Do you think that there might be more colours surrounding the outermost part of the flame? The one that is similar to a rainbow?"

"There might very well be more colours that are imperceptible to my eyes! Maybe one day I will see them! On the other hand, maybe there are no further bands of colours to be seen. I cannot give a definite answer to this question, not yet."

"I now understand your message to humanity and I also understand the parts of the flame and what it all means. There is something more that I want to understand now. Why do you believe that there is no 'religion of peace' or 'religion of love' or 'religion of truth'? Should it not be that the followers of religions be allowed to call their religions as they would like to?"

"I believe that there is no 'religion of peace' because the only religion of peace is Peace itself. There is no 'religion of love' because the only religion of love is Love itself. There is no 'religion of truth' because the only religion of truth is Truth itself. These that we seek and are promised to us by followers of various religions, can be found within ourselves! The Kingdom is Within!

If you want to find peace, then be Peaceful. If you want to find love, then be Loving. If you want to find truth, then be Truthful. Seek Peace, seek Love and seek Truth— within yourself.

Nobody needs to follow anything that anyone says in order to find those treasures promised by those people. Those treasures may be (and should be) born within yourself. So if you want your religion to be Peace, then draft your own Creed that is Peaceful! If you want your religion to be Love, then draft your own Creed that is Loving. If you want your religion to be Truth, then live by a Creed that seeks Truth in all things. Then you may say, 'My religion *is* Peace', 'My religion *is* Love', 'My religion *is* Truth.' The Treasure itself should be your religion! Not the words or the ways that are supposed to tell you how to reach the Treasures. The Treasures are *within you!*

It is remarkable how we have all been taught to not search for a Soul Mate outside of ourselves (not to search for The One who will complete us); and yet, we are simultaneously taught to search for those Treasures that are within us— outside of ourselves! Why are we always taught the wrong? Another person that you seek— yes— search for them! And yes, they are another living being on the outside of yourself! Search for that person— yes! You can be completed by another— yes! But these Treasures that we are taught to search for in religions? No— these Treasures are found within ourselves! People are blind, then they lead others who are equally blind. What is within is taught to be sought without while what is without is taught to be sought within! What a gruesome deception.

Now you understand why I say what I say, don't you?"

"Yes, I do understand! But I want to know even more! If we were to simply have within ourselves that which we are accustomed to seeking on the outside of ourselves, how then may we produce zeal? How then may we produce the valuable fire of passion? Is passion not a fire that we must strive to conceive and to fan into greatness? Because if the Treasures are already Within, then why fan a flame that will push us all around to find these Treasures on the outside?"

"Zeal can be described as 'burning'. And yet burning leads to third-degree burns!

What is to be said about the objects in life that do not cause us to burn, yet are worthy of our utmost admiration? The very small things that bring joy, comfort, reassurance, happiness? Some people are so zealous that they prefer the term 'joy' over 'happiness', because, 'happiness' is supposed to be the shallow form of joy. So zealous that they cannot even be happy!

And what can be said of morality? Is morality overly thought about and pondered upon? Why do our own moral choices mean so much to us and why do the moral choices of others offend us in such great ways? Why do we place such zeal into our own morality and into the morality of others who are not going to be a part of our lives, anyway?

Perhaps it is time to let go of the word 'morality' and instead, live by the word 'creed'. Morality falls through all the time, anyway, because it is too much associated with the word 'hypocrite'. But Creed is different. Creed is something that you may draft and construct and live by, without employing the passions that are evoked by the actions of others in their own lives that have nothing to do with your own.

Perhaps it is time to let go of the word 'passion', along with all the favour this word has found in our eyes within our century. Instead, favour the word 'beauty' (a word which we have all been taught is shallow and that we should not care about). If a thought does not produce an end result of beauty— do not think of it! If a belief does not make the world a beautiful place to live in— stop believing in it. Regard beauty as the highest form of thought, belief and Faith. Why should you ever think, believe in, or have faith in what is not a cause for beauty?

Beauty, happiness... seek the simplicity! This is life unto the human race. Zeal is death, zeal is destruction.

I know that I have also taught you before that we must burn and burn until we have died so much that we will finally begin to live. I know I have said that to you before. Nevertheless, it is very difficult for people to maintain a balance within themselves, making it very necessary for me to create the balance through my words, myself.

It is good to burn until you have died to the life that is not even living. But it is wrong to burn until you have died to the life that you were supposed to live; it is wrong to burn until you have burned your life away into the grave; it is wrong to burn until you burn away all the beauty around you! It is wrong to burn until you have burned away this gift called Life that has been given to you. Burn to burn away the death around you— yes. But only for that. Burn with Love for someone, burn with desire for a craft, burn with the zest of waking up to a beautiful new morning! Yes, yes and yes. But I do not tell you that you need to burn your life away!

I envision a race of people who draft their own Creeds and live by them, then find others who share in their Creed! I envision a race of people not easily swayed by zeal and by passion, but I envision humankind as seekers of simple beauty in everyday life. Seekers of beauty within the Soul, outside of the Soul, in others and around others. Seekers of simplicity. *Not all that burns creates diamonds and not all that does not burn will not shine!"*

"Are you saying though, that zeal in itself is a cause for death and is evil?"

"No, that is not what I am saying. But the inception of a zealous thought into the mind can mature into death and destruction. On the other hand, it could also mature into great and wonderful things. Zeal is neutral, but what you are zealous about can very quickly escalate into hatred. The relationship between hatred and zeal is very close. When I say, 'zeal is death, zeal is destruction', the purpose of that is to plant a seed of the opposite nature, because I know that if I plant a seed of the opposite nature of what is being cultivated in the world right now, then I will be providing the balance which is very much needed right now!

We have plenty of inceptions of the thought that zeal is the utmost reach of a person; that without passion, nothing is worthwhile doing, nothing is worthwhile staying for or sticking with. This results in many broken families and irresponsible citizens. You see, at the turn of the century, there began a movement to fan the flame of passions. Passion was suddenly the driving force of man.

It has taken many decades to reach the point where humanity has now gone overboard, but it has in fact happened. On a domestic scale, we see people unsatisfied with their relationships the moment they no longer feel like they are 'burning'. Or they leave their jobs if it is not their 'true heart's desire', regardless of the fact that their true heart's desire won't feed their children. These are just some examples. The new teaching at the turn of the century is now a very widespread way of life and it has destroyed many things at this point of oversaturation. In order to change this at this point in time, a new seed of thought must be planted to counteract the old and established one. And I believe this seed is the seed of neutrality and simplicity. *Not all that comes from the furnace is diamond and not all without fire does not shine.*

We also have plenty of seeds planted, of the thought that the inner fire will take one to paradise and that one should not be afraid of death, must be a martyr for one's faith. The small joys of being alive are thrown away by this growing thought in the mind of the zealot. This has been the cause of many murders and many acts of terrorism in the world, today.

There are many seeds of zeal already planted, that outright advocate zeal as being the utmost goal to reach for. To counter these seeds, there must be an equally powerful seed planted: the clear vision that zeal will very easily and very quickly take away rather than give. Only by the inception of this thought, may we be able to fight the inception of its opposite and opposing nature.

Every single day, people of this world are bombarded by directions unto passion. 'Leave your job if it does not kindle the fire within you'. 'Leave your partner if there is no fire burning between you'. So on and so forth. 'Do not worry about life if your life is painful to you; it is only the burning fire of your religion that will bring you into a beautiful afterlife'! Messages of passion bombard everyone, every day. Why would it be so bad to entertain a message of the opposite nature? There is no balance in this world! I am injecting the balance needed.

I mentioned the pendulum earlier; it is a pendulum that swings back and forth and has been doing so all throughout history. From the left to the right to the left to the right to the left to the right… I have mentioned to you the importance of neutrality. Why is neutrality necessary? Is neutrality the absence of passions, entirely? Or is neturality really the ability to place passions in the place where they need to belong in order to create balance? The ability to place weight where weight is needed.

When a soul attaches to the surface of things without the ability to penetrate within them, then there will be fragments of soul left scattered all about the object. But when a soul is able to immediately penetrate into the midst of a thing without attaching and scattering itself all about it, it naturally follows that the soul is able to remove itself quickly, as well, without remnants of itself left all around. Of course, the "objects" of mention here are events, concepts, circumstances, ideals, et al. In this way, the soul embodies the qualities of a double-edged sword able to pierce where it should pierce. Like an arrow able to penetrate the center of the eye.

Imagine yourself stirring a great lake, given the task to stir the lake first to the left and then to the right, then to continue with this stirring from left to right, until a certain balance is reached, until a certain flavouring is reached. The goal is to eventually gain the skill to stir the lake in such a way that it neither shifts to left nor to right; rather, it should attain enough equilibrium that it stands still. *Equilibrium*. This is not an easy task, hence, this has not been achieved on a worldwide scale since civilisation came into being.

Imagine yourself watching the golden pendulum and the goal is for it to finally reach a state where it no longer swings, but it lingers in the middle: equilibrium, balance! Miniscule oscillations between left and right, at a constant pace, are necessary to attain stillness, balance. We have watched this pendulum swing from far left to far right and back again, since time immemorial. Some have watched and have determined when the pendulum swing should be stopped in its path and should be turned into the opposite direction. It is necessary to be keen, to observe, to listen. If the direction of swinging is not reversed in time, the bob will hit the wall and when the wall falls, this signifies the destruction of civilisation. Many times, civilisations have fallen! Then the pendulum goes into swing, again.

The Fire Keeper is not the pendulum; nevertheless, the Fire Keeper knows the ways of the pendulum. Within the pendulum there are wheels that control the system. It is not the task of the Fire Keeper to ride with the flow upon these wheels, rather, it is the task of the Fire Keeper to ride on the Higher Wheel, to conform to the turning of the Higher Wheel, which is a turning that produces equilibrium. When the turning of the Higher Wheel goes against the turnings of the lower wheels in the pendulum, it is the task of the Fire Keeper to remain in the Higher Wheel, while the lower wheels of the pendulum are naturally forced into submission (not through your own efforts; rather, by the natural movement of the Higher Wheel).

"How does one remain in this constant balance?"

"You are to remain in this balance by placing the weights of your various passions into the places where they are needed, in order to create equilibrium in the pendulum. Do not be dedicated *to your* passions; instead, *you* dedicate your passions *to where* they must be placed. Of course, there are the things that are to never be replaced, misplaced or moved and these are those things listed in the Creed of the Dragon, these are the results of Love and the objects of Love's loyalty and affections. The Dragon Creed is the Law of the Higher Wheel and this law we do not go against.

The Dragon Creed is the turning of the Higher Wheel, the balance of Darkness and Light; therefore, we do not stray from it.

The simple vision to keep in mind, is that you must not be so dedicated to an ideal that you remove yourself from life, in the process. I have seen this too often. Life removed from man and woman in the process of their dedication to an ideal. The dedication to an ideal is identified as passion for it. People lay down their lives (mentally, physically and emotionally), giving up peace, harmony and joy in the process of pledging allegiance to an ideal. Sometimes, the passion is for passion, itself! They have said, "Give up all things that do not burn with passion", and in doing so, these people have not even dedicated their passions to a thing or to a person; instead, they have dedicated their bodies, minds and hearts to (their idea of) passion, itself! I cannot think of anything more destructive than this. They are led like blind mules unto the edge of a cliff and then pushed over that cliff! I cannot think of anything more destructive to relationships, to family and to friendships, to the home. We must be Master of our passions, never blind mules led by what we believe passion is and where we believe it is leading us. Fire rises and bends; should we be led by the rising and the bending of the Fire, or should we master the Fire and determine where to place it, determine when to rise and to bend, when to bow low and to reach high, just like the Flame, itself?

When a flame bows low, do we say of this flame, that it is lost of all purpose and must be extinguished? Or do we know that it will rise high again in a few seconds? The people are weak because they are taught not the nature of the Flame itself, but only taught to look for a raging fire and to extinguish a quiet one. But the quiet fire will rage again, will rise again. Should we be mere spectators of the Fire, misinterpreting where we think it leads us? Or should we be the Fire, itself, understanding its movements? Should we be mere participants in the nature of the Flame, only dancing where we are placed, or should we be Masters of the Fire, determining where to place our Flame? We must be both Flame and Master of the Flame, just as we are who our Mind is, at the same time, we ought to become the Master of that Mind."

"What can be said of the fact that you are teaching about Fire, and yet, you are now speaking down the very Flames that you have mastered? I am confused!"

"Nay, you are of little understanding! It is because I have mastered the Flame, that I know when it bows and when it rises; that I know its twists and turns— how it dances! The one who is ignorant of the Flame only imagines a fire that burns and burns! The one who has mastered the Flame knows the nature of it. Flame bows and rises, it gives way and it dances. It has many states. To Master the Flame, is to Master *all* states of it. To Master the Flame, is to be One with the Flame— to know when to bow and when to rise, when to dance and when to give way! And very importantly— where to place the Flame in all of its dancing! It is because I am Master of the Flame that I say these things. It is because I am One with the Flame that I teach you these things! Try to keep up, you of little understanding."

"I am thankful that I have you, because with you, I am not just of little understanding, but I am also you all the same! But tell me more, I am curious, what can be said of religion in relation to zeal? It seems as though you are alluding to zeal being a dangerous force in religion. How are we to plant the seed to fight the seeds that have already been planted?"

"This is the seed that we must plant, that a person should never identify first and foremost with a religion. A person should never forget that he or she is living in a physical body and that he or she is, in fact, a person; not only an adherent of his or her religion.

To have Faith is good. To have faith beyond the identification of the self is wrong. What about you? Do you identify first and foremost with your religion? What is the color of your eyes, what are your dreams at night? What makes you laugh? What do you want to be tomorrow, ten years from now? Many things are you. Your religion is not you.

Everybody needs to draw this line in the sand and be like, 'That over there is the religion that I subscribe to, it was developed some few thousand years ago and I happen to believe in its teachings.' And then look at your side of the line in the sand and say, 'This here is me, a person with dreams and hopes. I like to eat oatmeal in the morning, I like strawberries.'

This identification with religion as a person is wrong. People are filled with too much zeal, people forget they are people and forget that other people are also people, all for a passion in the soul!

Passion of the Soul is a dime a dozen. It is not what they would want you to believe it is! Everyone has it. It is not glorified, it is not anything. You know what's something? The little things are something. They don't even have to make you burn! The smiles of your loved ones, the way the Sun sets and the Moon rises. The flowers and the way they bloom...

these are somethings. Beauty! There is too much Beauty thrown away in the name of passion. There are too many moments of reflection that are lost because people no longer see themselves reflected in anything other than their religions!

That is the seed we must plant, which will fight the seeds that have already been planted. It is unfortunate that humankind is incapable of creating balance on her own. We must create balance for her. Dragons must create balance for the people. We must plant these seeds that will grow into the crawling vines that will choke the poisonous ones which have already been long growing. The new goal now is neutrality. The new aim now is neutrality. The aim of previous decades and of our whole century has been the kindling of passions. That ambition has been reached and has gone overboard. The new vision of the next era must be a vision of neutrality if we are to mend the brokenness that this era's vision has already caused in the world. Imagine a people so neutral that they are not stirred into hatred. You could say that this is a fearsome thing to imagine, because if people are not stirred unto hatred, this also means that they will not be stirred unto Love. That thought though, is just another erroneous lie being fed to the masses. They have taught everyone that hate closely resembles Love. What an absolutely obvious lie. Hate does not resemble Love! Listen to yourself say that hate resembles Love, and then laugh at yourself for even saying it! Hate *does not* resemble Love.

Moreover, they have told everyone that fear is the opposite of Love; I laugh at this outright lie! Fear is oftentimes found adjacent to Love, because we fear so much to lose those whom we Love. They have also told you that if you fear to lose the ones you Love, that is not true Love. I laugh at this! Are you not afraid that your mother or father will die? Has this not been a long held fear since you were a child? Does this therefore mean that you do not actually Love your mother and/or father, because of the fact that you fear to lose him/her/them? Why do people so readily believe what they are told, when these things told to them are very obviously distortions of truth and outright lies? Why? Anyhow, it does not matter why! What matters is that it is the case!

God forbid that your mother or father die, by the way. We do not wish that, at all. It is true that we fear to lose those whom we Love and that is why fear is often found alongside Love. And to fear losing those whom we Love, does *not* mean that we actually do not Love them! Please be rid of this lie! What a load of rubbish all people have been taught! Unnatural rubbish! It is only natural to fear losing those whom you Love.

Hate does not resemble Love. Hate is the opposite of Love, while fear is oftentimes found alongside Love. And sometimes, the more we Love a person, the more we fear losing him/her. This is the natural Truth.

People have been taught unnatural ways and as a result, they have learned how to run away from the natural occurrences that accompany Love. And so they abandon people who Love them. They abandon people who Love them, over and over again; because they believe a lie and in the belief of their lie, they are actually convinced that they possess superior knowledge! Because they read it in a book or heard it from a speaker!

Look at me! I read no books, I listen to no speakers! What am I doing then? I am simply witnessing the effects of their teachings upon the billions of people in the world and I wish to fight it. Why do I wish to fight it, when it is of no effect in my own life? I wish to fight it because I have offspring in this world and I have seen that this world is not good enough for my offspring! I lament the fact that I bring Souls into a world that is not good enough for them. And so, what should I do about this? I should change the world that they live in, that is what I should do!"

"Are you saying that all you do is an act of Love for the children you have brought and will bring into this world?"

"Yes, that is exactly what I am saying."

"All you do, you do because of the fact that you are a mother?"

"Yes. We become mothers long before our children are born, do you know that? We are already their mothers. And when they come into this world, that is the physical part of the journey. But before we brought them into this world, we were already sharing a journey with them, though it was still unseen to the physical eye. As such, our relationships wth our children are all unique, Divine, and tailored to ourselves and to them. We cannot truly compare ourselves to other mothers and this is why there is no true handbook to parenting. Because my journey as a mother is not yours and your journey as a parent is not mine. Our journeys as parents are as individual as the people who we are and as unique as the people who our children are. Our journeys began long before this corporeal body existed and will continue beyond it.

I cannot emphasise enough the fact of how much we absolutely need each other. We need the other half of us and we need our families. We need our parents, our children and they need us. We need. In this life, we need. We were born needy and we will die in need of those who will lay us into the ground. With this knowledge in mind, can you even begin to imagine how sinister it is, that we are all being taught that we ought to spend every waking hour of our precious lives believing that 'we are the universe', 'we need no one', 'we are our own soul mates' and 'we are whole on our own'? It is an absolutely sinister teaching. If one were to believe such teachings, then there are only two times when one has truly lived their life: first is when they were born and second is when they die! Two moments of epiphany and in the middle of all that— nothing! Oh dear God, have mercy on the human race!"

"Before I ask more about being a mother and a parent, I want to clarify something first: have you actually told me that fear and Love are on the same level and of equal importance? Is that what you mean by saying that fear is oftentimes found alongside Love?"

"Absolutely not! Fear and Love are *not* of the same importance and are *not* on the same level. In fact, Love should overcome the Fear that often accompanies it. Fear gives Love its depth and strength; in that it is the crucible that Love overcomes and in doing so, Love emerges stronger, more fortified. However, this is not to say that they are of equal importance and that if you do not Fear the loss, then you cannot have a strong and fervent Love.

Nevertheless, on a personal note, it would be difficult for me to believe that someone Loves me if that person is not afraid of losing me. I simply would not be able to confirm Love, if I cannot see in their eyes that they cannot imagine their lives without me."

"Are you afraid of losing those whom you Love?"

"Yes, I am. I am not afraid in the sense that I fear imminent danger, but I am afraid in the sense of someone who Loves and fears to lose whom she Loves. I am also afraid of being lost from the ones whom I Love. My life is not only lived for me; my life I live for them, too."

"If Fear has this relationship with Love, then how can Fear be evil in nature? Is not something evil in nature, evil in all things? How can an evil thing be at sometimes beneficial and at most times hazardous?"

"When we study the biology of fear, we will see that fear did not develop as a hazard; rather, fear developed in order to protect from hazards! Fear in biology is, in fact, the reason why our human species has been capable of surviving era after era; generation after generation. Without fear, we would not be here today as a species.

The physical applications of fear are valuable. And when I say physical, what I mean is biological. It is when we go into fear as applied to psychology that we begin to see it as a hazard rather than a benefit. And when I say psychology, I mean the mind. Not the brain, but the mind: the aspect that is not physical, not biological. Fear in the arena of the intangible becomes harmful because it can easily overtake your outlooks in life. Your daily life can, in fact, become so tainted by fear, that your reality actually becomes distorted and you begin to see reality in a different light, which has been tainted by fear. And by a different light, I mean a negative light. What is negative? Negative is the force that creates undesirable outcomes.

Nevertheless, when it comes to Love and Fear, we can say that Love exists in the arena of the intangible, but then there sits Fear alongside it! This is a mystery. I have explained to you so many mysteries; and yet, this one is a mystery that I cannot explain. Maybe Love is both tangible and intangible and that is why Fear with Love is both beneficial and harmful. It is beneficial in that it can confirm Love and it can give strength to Love; but then it can also cause you to never find Love in the first place if it is stronger than your desire to overcome it! Someone who cannot overcome their fears cannot find Love, for the sheer fear of it! Therefore, to the both tangible and intangible Love, Fear can be either beneficial or hazardous. I guess you can say that Love is that sphinxlike essence which walks with one foot in this world and one foot in the next world. In one world, Fear is an asset and in the other, Fear is a hazard!"

"Which is a greater love? A love for the world or a love for one's nation?"

"The world is like the human body. When you look at the human body, you see a single biological system covered in one giant field of skin. You can tell me that there are no borders on my body; but inside my body, there is a skeletal system, a muscular system, a nervous system; there are tissues, cells... there are plenty of little communities working together as a whole, in order for my body to function. They are all different, but they are connected. My heart is not my lung and my eyes are not my ears. Each part needs to be different in order for me to be a fully functional human being. What would happen if my eyes decided to be just like my ears? What would happen if my fingers wanted to be just like my toes? Then I would be a deformed and dysfunctional human being.

You cannot tell me that in this world we need to all be the same because to tell me that would be telling me that you want the world to be dysfunctional and deformed. Yes, when the Earth is looked upon from a spacecraft, you are not going to see where a country ends and where it begins. But that is just like looking at my body from the outside. You need to go in to see what's inside.

In order for a body to function, all parts must be in harmony and undivided. If you were to divide my heart in half, I would cease to live. In this same exact light, if you are to divide a nation in half, expect not the world to unite. The only way for the world to unite is for the nations to unite first within themselves. The only way for a community to unite is for the families to unite first within themselves. Do not tell me about the inexistence of nations in a plea to unite the whole world. The whole world will never unite, until you as a nation first heal yourself.

A love for the world, is equal in importance to a love for one's nation. A love for one's nation is equivalent in importance to a love for this world. But you cannot possibly love the world, if you do not love your nation. You can say that you are a 'citizen of the world' and what not; but these are all just words! Do not bring a man to me who does not know how to feed his own children and then tell me that I should trust him to feed mine! Do not bring me a woman who does not know how to be faithful to her partner and then tell me that she will be faithful to my son!

You cannot Love the world, until you have Loved your nation. You cannot heal the world, until you have healed your own community. You cannot feed my children until you have fed your own. You cannot call this planet your own home when your own home is still under renovation.

Each member of the world (each nation), is loving the world by loving itself! To do the best with your own, is to do the best in a small part of this big world. Like a diseased body— if you rot— you are a cause for sickness in the rest of the world. So, make sure you are healthy, make sure you are happy, make sure that you build up your children towards a brighter future, guiding them in the way they should go. To Love yourself is to Love the World. To Help yourself is to Help the world. To rise up in this world, is to take a portion of this planet up into the sky with you. As you do for yourself, so you have done for everyone.

Is this to say that you should turn a blind eye to those who are suffering? Undeniably, there are those who have less and there are those who suffer. If you turn away from them and focus on your own benefits, is this the great Love that I speak of? No. That is not so. Help in the ways that you are able to help and help as much as you can! Do not ever turn a blind eye! But in the event that the suffering is too great of a thing for you to handle and in the event that the help needed is too great for you to bear without breaking, then you must let the cycles of nature take their course. As people die and are born, nations also die and are born. Sometimes, the death of a nation cannot be prevented. In such cases, nature will take its course. Like amputation, it is better to remove the decaying matter than to allow the decay to spread to all areas of the body. Is it better to allow a whole person to die because one finger has become infected beyond repair? Or is it better to remove that one finger?"

"It is, of course, better to remove the one finger."

"We are not to abandon a world in need; however, we are to realise that to break ourselves for another, is to break a greater part of this world. If you truly love this world, then you will see that you cannot continue to break it by breaking your own nation.

If you are married or are committed to someone whom you Love and who Loves you, then you are One and you break and mend with one another, as One. But this is a Sacred Love, this is a different kind of Love. It is crucial and essential for everyone, everywhere, to realise that there are different types of Love, not all are the same! Even in Love, we cannot give equal proportions to everyone! If we were to give equal and same kind of Love to everyone that we meet, then how would our families remain sacred, how would our relationships remain sacred, how would our homes remain sacred? We see the breaking up of families because people cannot tell the difference between the different types of Loves that ought to be given!"

"What about when it comes to parents and children? Is it better to love oneself over one's child?"

"Undeniably and unquestionably, I will always Love my children more than I Love myself. And I would rather break myself than see any of my children broken. But this is a Sacred Love that is Family. Family is where the greatest amount of Love must relish and must thrive.

It is because of my children, that I turned to loving this world! If not for my becoming a mother, I would not have ever thought to change the world!"

"Why do you say 'children' instead of 'child'? Do you consider other people to all be your children?"

"No, I do not consider other people to all be my children. But I consider all the children of mine that have not yet been born to me, to be my children right now before they have even been born. That is why I say, children, even if now I have only one child born to me."

"A mother's Love knows not the concept of space nor of time?"

"A mother's Love, similar to the Love of a Soul Mate, heeds no concept of space nor no concept of time. A mother's Love, similar to the Love of a true

Soul Mate, goes beyond the existence of the physical body. My children that have not yet been born—they are already my children, along with the one who has already been born to me. That is why I say 'children'."

"How can things that do not exist, already be real? And how can things that are not yet real, already exist?"

"What makes you think that we are already certain of what is real and what is not real? Or of what exists and what does not exist? What about the future? You are not there yet, but does that mean it does not exist? What about the past? You are no longer there, but does that mean it never did exist? We must not limit ourselves by what we have already designated as reality, what we have already designated as fact.

I happen to believe that the future is already there and that my future self is already there. I also happen to believe that we may change the past (the past is not fixed). So really, would it be so surprising if I also believe that my children are already my children even before they have been born into the world? I believe that they know me and that I know them."

"What is the most important thing to remember in order to be a good parent, a good mother, a good father?"

"I think that the most important thing to remember is that parenting is about *knowing* your children. Parenting is about knowing *who* that person is— your child— and then sharing with them a life, being a part of theirs and they being a part of yours. They say that we don't choose our children and that we don't choose our parents, but I believe that we actually do. There are reasons. And we can find those reasons.

They say the way to be a good parent is to read good books and follow good rules. But I say that to be a good parent is to have a good relationship with another person— that person being your child, those people being your children. *Know* them. *Feel* them.

Be in a *relationship* with your children. *That* is how to be a good parent.

We start new relationships when we bring new people into the world. So why don't we treat them as such? Parenting is not a 'method' or a 'style'. Parenting is not a 'way of life' or a 'fashion'. Parenting is a Love, a Devotion, a Life. Not a life's style; but a Life. Being a parent is not like choosing a style of clothing to wear and then saying, that from now on, this is you, this is what you want people to see you as, this is the life you want to live... but rather, it is like meeting new people for the first time: loving them, keeping them there, staying with them and them staying with you. Except you Love them more than just any other person."

"Is it essential to be in Love with the person who helped you conceive your child?"

"The answer to that depends on the person, it really does. There are people who become parents through adoption, through artificial insemination... for them, it is not essential to be in Love with the person who helped them conceive their child or have their child.

However, I know what you are asking, you are asking if it is essential for two people who say they are in love, to really be in Love when they bring children into the world. I wouldn't say that it is 'essential' because to say that it is 'essential' is to say that a child cannot be brought into the world and brought up as their child, at all, unless they are in Love! So, I won't say that it is essential, but I *will* say that it is an incredibly vital and life-giving ingredient. Children conceived in absolute Love, have a very beautiful gift intertwined into the fabric of their bodies. Notwithstanding, there are many children conceived outside of Love, that are given very special gifts by the Gods, out of mercy and out of favour for no other reason than that they are favoured— it is a beautiful thing to witness!"

"We live in a big world that is today filled with so much violence and hatred. It seems like the more people struggle for 'enlightenment' and 'oneness', the deeper they fall into violence, resentment, hatred. This is puzzling to my mind, it is so ironic. Shouldn't the violence diminish with the onslaught of sameness and oneness? And yet, the opposite is the case. Tell me, how can all parents raise their children to become people who will be able to change the world one day? What can parents teach their children, so that the future can be a better place for them?"

"Teach your children this from a very early age: 'Everybody in this world is different, you're going to meet people who don't look like you, think like you, or even feel like you. This world is filled with so many different colours and shapes, so many different thoughts and feelings. You should never expect anyone else to be the same as you and you should never expect yourself to be the same as anybody else. But everyone can have so much fun learning about each other and celebrating one another' and when you are all able to tell this to your children and implement this teaching in a way that makes them truly understand it, the world will begin to change for the better.

You see, nobody really understands racism. The problem of racism does not occur because people think others are different from themselves. The problem of racism occurs because people expect others to be the same as themselves and they are distraught when this is not true. And they will always be distraught because it will never be true. To tell people that we are all the same is to blatantly lie. No two people are the same. Not even twins are entirely the same. People need to be taught to expect differences in everyone. Seeing difference is not racism. Seeing difference is seeing reality! Celebrating difference is celebrating nature. Trying to kill all notion of differences is trying to kill nature. So what happens? Nature dies! People die.

I have always warned that the movement of sameness and 'we are oneness' is a belief system that produces bad fruit. I believe it is a delusional, deceptive and even hypocritical belief system. All these people convincing themselves that when they look out into the world, they see themselves as 'one' with everybody else; meanwhile, they cannot even manage to be one with their spouses or their partners at home. People want a whole world to be one; meanwhile, they find it impossible to reconcile with their family members. If I were to reach a point in my life when I would say 'I am one with everybody else', you can be sure that at such a point in time, I would be one with my partner/spouse, with my family and my friends. When everything is perfect in my own personal life and I have absolutely no negative feelings towards anyone within my own immediate circle, at that point in time I would have the right to look out into the world and believe that all I see is sameness and oneness. How can we contrive and attempt to live in a world that we cannot even build for ourselves within us?

People always want to project their ideals onto the world; ideals which they themselves cannot reach. In doing so, people attempt to live in an unreal state. It will never happen in reality. The only thing that will ever become real in this world, is what every person will be capable of doing within themselves and at home with their families. Broken people and broken relationships projecting their ideals of perfection onto the rest of the world, producing an illusion that will forever be unattainable, is a sad state to behold.

If we want the future to be a better place for our children, then we need to begin teaching them the opposite theory of what we are today always taught, we need to go against that flow. We need to teach our children to celebrate the many differences that they will see between themselves and others when they go to school; when they go out into the world. If every individual in the future meets every other person on the street in an expantancy of differences and in an attitude that is ready to celebrate those very differences: this would reduce the violence, misunderstandings, resentment and hate in all societies on our planet.

Today, we are taught to love all others equally to the way we love ourselves. But how do we love ourselves? Do we even love ourselves? Or our own? How do you love the people given to you whom you are to be One with? How do you love your spouse, your children? How do you love your family, your friends? Look to yourself and to yours first. Learn to Love yourself and yours first. Then when you are able to celebrate yourself and celebrate your own, with a true Love that is long-suffering and dedicated, only then will you be ready to Love others in such a way that you idealise.

Teach your children to celebrate the reasons why they are different, and no, they do not need to all 'become one'. Your religion does not need to become my religion, your favourite food does not need to become my favourite food, your favourite nail polish doesn't need to be mine. We can love one another despite our differences, while accepting those differences and celebrating the fact that they are there."

"How does the Fire, Love? What does Fire teach us about Loving someone?"

"I'm happy to hear you ask me this because the answer is beautiful! Fire Loves in a way that knows your every movement! When you hold a candle between your hands, watch the flame respond to you as you breathe. The flame will move back and forth, up and down, entirely responsive to your breathing. The flame between your hands knows your breath as it knows itself; it knows your body as it knows its own body. This is how Flame Loves. If you Love the way that Flame does, you Love as if the other body is your own; as if the other's breath is your own breath! You feel the movements, you react to the movements, you know what the other person means; you know what the other person feels and you move to that, you respond to that. To Love as the Flame Loves, is to MAKE LOVE to the one you Love, even when there is no sexual intercourse!"

"If that is the Love that Fire knows, then I can imagine that a Dragon cannot be Loved by any less than another Dragon! For how can one who has known that kind of Love, ever settle for anything other than it?"

"Indeed, Dragons are best Loved by Dragons. Fire is best Loved by Fire. Imagine knowing a Love like this, but then trying to replace it with anything else other than.

Fire also Loves in the way which burns away all that is not supposed to be there. In Love, there are many feelings, memories, unforgiveness, resentment… so much rubbish that gets itself in the middle, like how moulds get into the middle of a crack; but by the nature of Fire, this all burns away!

Fire can burn away not only the stuff that is not supposed to be in between Lovers, but also the stuff that is not supposed to be within yourself, anymore. When you Love yourself with the fiery warmth that is your Soul, you burn away all that is not supposed to be in yourself, anymore! To be Fire is to be able to burn away; to Love as Fire Loves, is to be able to Love while burning away the things that are not supposed to be there in the midst of that Love. You make yourself into Diamond; you make your Love into Diamond."

"In your brief description of lovemaking, you have made it sound as though it is of astronomical significance. This makes me wonder, how magical is sex? How important is it to have sex, to make love?"

"Lovemaking is one of the most important, enjoyable aspects of being in a human body. In fact, if it were entirely up to me and I were given the option to become human again just to enjoy sexual intercourse, I would! This is not to say that other beings do not have sexual intercourse, or that Gods do not have sexual intercourse. But this is to say that if I, as a soul, were given the opportunity to enjoy sexual intercourse in another area of existence (this physical planet that human beings live on), I would jump at the opportunity if only for the enjoyment of it! In that very same light, I can honestly say with genuine conviction, that I am not promiscuous. I can go without sexual intercourse for decades if I have not found someone worthy of me. The pleasure of the act does not destroy the worth of it. Do you understand that? True pleasure does not destroy worth and true desire for pleasure does not destroy the worth of what it so desires.

Sexual intercourse is so desirable that it is worth an incarnation, but to throw around that desire onto just anyone or any chance that comes along, would be destroying the worth of it, thus, reducing the value of it. A Dragon never reduces the value of anything that is worthy and valuable. As Keeper of Treasures, it is against the nature of the Dragon to reduce the value of an act, an object, a person, a thought, a desire. It is in this light that I am able to say that on the one hand, lovemaking is one of the utmost desirable acts of being human; but on the other hand, this does not mean that reducing the worth of it is justified by its desirability.

The prosaic are very different from us, especially in this aspect. They will haggle the worth of anything, in order to give as less as they can, for as much as they can receive. Remember what it is like to be at a weekend marketplace: there you are able to witness people haggling the value of everything for sale. A man will see something that he really likes, but then he will act as though he does not really like it *that* much, for the chance of getting away with giving the least amount that he can possible give, for it. Observe the woman at the marketplace who spots the most pefectly ornate porcelain vase, she has been looking for it, for years now! Instead of saying to the seller, 'I have been looking for this exact item for many years and I am delighted to find it here'; she will say, 'Oh I think this is good enough, but there is a crack here and a crack there...the colour is a bit off... I'll take it for half the price'.

Society and relationships are all played by the prosaic as they would play at the weekend marketplace. They are not cognizant of the fine line in the sand that separates 'thing' from 'human', from 'relationship', from 'Love'. The prosaic will haggle the worth of a partner, an experience, a feeling... as if Life itself is merely one big weekend marketplace! Alas, we witness the grostesque lack of discernment.

To us Dragons, that line in the sand separating 'thing' from 'person' is incredibly discernable. It is *so* discernable to us, that if we were to cross it, we would burn our own Souls in the process. A Dragon does not haggle the worth of another person, nor does a Dragon allow him or her self to be haggled with, by another person. We do not reduce the worth of that which we desire. We will not settle. We will have the whole value of that which we desire, for the full price of it. That is Dragon.

It is against the nature of the Dragon to ever say, 'Oh I did it because I couldn't take the temptation, the thought of the pleasure was just too much for me to handle.' The Dragon is slave to no one, *especially* not to its own flesh!"

"Tell me, explain to me, what actually happens when you make love? When a person makes love to another person, what is really happening, what is really going on? You explained to me about the Fire and how it makes love to the Air… what about a person and when he or she makes love to another person?"

"I cannot explain to you what happens between two people because it is a mundane area. But I can certainly explain to you what happens between two Dragons making Love. 'Two become One' is the simplest, most fulfilling statement that can be made to describe the act. The best time to send a message to your partner is during an orgasm. An orgasm is not simply and only for pleasure, the orgasm is for weaving together perfect bonds of connection between the two who are Making Love and to weave these bonds together in such a way that they are unbreakable. Not even the laws of physics may interact with these bonds; rather, these bonds will dictate the laws of physics around them.

There is such a thing in the world of quantum physics, that proves there are particles which, after an initial interaction with one another, become so entangled together, that nothing— absolutely nothing— not time, space, existence or even inexistence, is capable of coming in between them! In the field of quantum physics, this is called *quantum entanglement*. Experiments have been conducted by quantum physicists and theoretical physicists, which have proven that even the inexistence of one particle does not break the bonds initially created between itself and another. In other words, one being dead and the other being alive cannot even come in between the bonds created!"

"This is the most fascinating thing that I have ever, ever heard! Tell, me, how do these bonds manifest and how were scientists able to prove them?"

"It truly is the most fascinating thing that you have ever heard, because it is perhaps the most fascinating reality in existence. I could explain the experiments to you and I could name the scientists, but then this conversation would begin to sound like a scientific paper. Instead, you may find these things out through your own research, you only need to dig a little bit and you will find the technical details.

It suffices to say that scientists have their apparatus for conducting out-of-this-world experiments for the purpose of investigating theories. When probing into the theory of quantum entanglement , a team of scientists was indeed able to prove that even the expiry of one of the particles (the inexistence of one), would not alter the effect that the other could have on it. In very simple terms, if you were to poke particle A with a beam of blue light, particle B would be able to not only feel the poke, but would be able to actually see the color of the beam of light used (blue). And this is regardless of whether or not particle B exists according to the standards of existence experienced by particle A. This is regardless of whether or not Particle B is on the opposite end of the galaxy, inside of a black whole, or even on the other end of the universe! According to Karl Tate over at LiveScience, *The transfer of state between Photon A and Photon B takes place at a speed of at least 10,000 times the speed of light, possibly even instantaneously, regardless of distance.*

When Dragons form bonds during orgasm, these bonds are the workings of quantum entanglement. Keep in mind though, that this is not to say that sexual intercourse and orgasm is the only way that Two may become One. It may actually happen the very first time you both lay eyes upon one another: old bonds reform, rebond and take immediate root."

"Tell me though, how can anything 'reform, rebond and take immediate root' if it has not previously happened?"

"Time, distance, outcome, future, past and present do not exist on the terms of our experience of existence and of what is reality or unreality. Do you think that these great laws bend to us? Nay, they do not bend to us; rather, we bend to what we believe in. *We bend to what we believe in.*

To say that I may bend these laws, in actuality, is saying that I am bending the laws that other people have adapted to and believe in. It is saying that I am bending what you perceive as reality and what you perceive as normal and acceptable and commonplace— not because I am changing the actual nature of these, but because I am actually in sync with the True nature of these. As they have said long ago, Magic is not supernatural; rather, Magic is natural. To know Magic is to know the natural, to know nature. Why did they say these things? Those things have been said, because what people know, in general, is not natural. People know their own weird version of reality that is not natural but they label it as natural. The True nature of things is what they would label as Magic. A Mage simply knows the Nature of things, thus, he is a Mage.

Is this to downplay the Beauty and the Power in being a Fire Gazer, in being a Dragon, in being a Master, a Mage? Is 'Natural' singing to a downplayed tune? Nay, this is not to downplay anything at all. This is in fact only to show you that the Nature of one is not the nature of the other. I may exist and know True Nature, while another exists and knows true nature. What is entirely Natural to one, may be entirely unnatural to the other. I am not even going to call unto all people and say, 'Come and listen to reality because I know reality and I live in what is only Natural and all of you are blinded, unnatural fools', I would not call unto people and tell them such things, only because I do not believe in doing so. Others do, but I do not. I speak from my own Nature, which may not be the nature of another. In such a case, why should I try to pull someone over to where I am standing, when they are supposed to be (or want to be) standing exactly where they are?

But to those who are of my Nature— I *do* call unto you. The laws of nature as they know them, do *not* need to dictate us. And now, back to your question: how can anything reform, rebond and reroot if it has not already done so before— well now, what makes you so sure that you can at any time be aware of the previous existence of a thing, or of the future existence or nonexistence of a thing? What makes you so sure that what you know to be reality *now*, is absolute reality for all and of all time? How do you know that a person you have met today, is not someone whom you met three hundred years ago in another place? You may have initially bonded then. You might have in fact died in each others' arms at the end of a very long life in a previous lifetime, promising to return again to seek the other out on this Earth, to live and to build a life with each other yet again! Maybe even again and again! Therefore, when I say 'reroot, reform, rebond'—yes, these may have already happened before, somewhere else. You could even be looking into the past from your futures (your present day might be an active participation of your future selves in past events), in order to direct and mould your journey towards the outcome that is already living and thriving in the future (what you think is the future, but is in actuality your present)."

"Today might actually be my past, tomorrow my present, and the future is not actually never there yet, because it is, in reality, the true 'present day'?"

"You have understood correctly. This may in fact be the case."

"And I could, in fact, be loving someone, for even more than a thousand years?"

"You could, in fact, be loving someone, for even more than two thousand years!"

"There are such possibilities that exist, or I could say, there is such an existence of possibilities; notwithstanding, people would rather be eaten up by trivialities and swallowed whole by things like the worries of reputation, of what others may think, of how to keep up with the neighbors? Alas, my eyes are witness to the stupidities of humankind!"

"Maybe they are stupid, but maybe they are just who/what they are supposed to be. I am not in favour of the notion that we must impose our knowledge and/or our experiences upon others who do not have the same. I am not even in favour of expecting others to have or to know the same as I! Their journeys will lead them to where they are supposed to be and if their journeys don't do that, it is not my responsibility to fix it. It is their own. My responsibility is to my children, to my Love, to my Own. If there are others who hear my song, they may follow me simply because I have a song; not because I must sing my song for them! If they are stupid, then they may remain stupid or they may change and become knowledgeable if it is their choice and if it is their path."

"Well, you may teach me as you wish, but I think that the majority of people are stupid and I do not mean curious and innocent; but I mean really, really stupid."

"I do think that the majority of people cannot see past the length of their outstretched arm. But this is just normal. What is stupid to us is simply normal in this world. They are prosaic. What is normal to the prosaic appears as stupidity to our eyes. Therefore, since we are the ones who are different, then we do not have a place from which to judge others as being stupid. They are not stupid here, they are in fact normal. Not being able to see past your own outstretched arm may appear to us as stupidity, but to them, it is just the way that they are. Instead of saying 'stupid', it is the graceful choice to say, 'they who cannot see further.' Yes, it is a longer thing to say, but time does not chase us around, we have the time to say a few words more than just one word.

Like I already said, how can a person determine what kind of a tree stands in front of him, if he cannot yet see the fruit? It is our nature to see the fruit first! But this is not their nature. It is their nature to see the tree and make conclusions about the fruit, but only to see the true outcome after the tree has bore its fruit. Is it really stupidity if a living thing is merely acting out of its own nature?

The nature of some is, in fact, lesser than the nature of others. But that is of no concern to us or to anybody except those of lesser nature. I do fully understand why many have the desire to teach, to show, to guide and to help. Many call themselves 'enlightened' or 'awakened'. They are convinced that it is their mission on this planet to in turn enlighten and awaken all those around them, in order to create a unified human race. Of course, there is only disappointment to be found in their methods. I fully understand their intentions, however, if we were to eradicate the Outer Flame, then we would also eradicate the Inner Flame, as I have already explained to you. In doing so we would, in fact, be undoing a good thing, instead of causing a good thing to grow and to take root.

On the other hand, there are some who are truly called to do just what they believe it is they should do in this world. We need to let them be. But then they also need to let others be.

"How can you teach others if you are to just let them be? The soul of teaching comes from the fact that you do not wish to let others just be!"

"Well, the key is to simply *be there*. You can 'show up' to 'be there' while at the same time letting others be.

A butterfly is simply there, a butterfly 'shows up' in the most elegant sense of the word. It flutters silently into the garden, making no noise, imposing not itself upon the garden; nevertheless, the beauty of its wings is able to light up an already flourishing place (or a dull place). It brings joy to the eyes, a smile to the face. It is small and light, yet people will stop and stare. I am not even sure if the butterfly wants to do that. It just is. We may say the same about dragonflies, too.

Teach from the overflow of the wine glass of life, do not teach from the desire to correct. Yes, we do have the desire to correct and in our case, this desire is justified. But this desire is best applied to correcting our own paths and the paths that are intermingled with our own, the people whom we Love, for example. Our desire to correct must come from the fact that we see the fruit and we wish to show the other what type of fruit the tree is bearing before the tree has actually bore it."

"How much should we desire to correct ourselves?"

"I am very glad that you have asked me this. It is all too easy to get carried away with correcting ourselves. Too often we forget to be gentle with ourselves and to Love our own selves the way that we are Loved by the Heavens. We may have the voice of the disciplinarian within us, this voice prunes us and pushes us, pinches us and commands us— in order to produce the best possible outcome for ourselves. The problem arises when we forget to speak to ourselves with the voice of the comforter, the one who comforts. If we speak to ourselves in the voice of the disciplinarian, we must also have within us the voice of the comforter, the soothsayer. Then, we must not only speak to ourselves in this comforting and soothing voice, but we must heed this gentle voice, as well.

I know that I must speak to my Soul as I would speak to an infant or a small child. I must reassure my Soul, I must comfort my Soul, appreciate myself, place value upon myself, caress the curvatures of my Soul and Mind with a touch that is soft and even beguiling. For inside me thrives an infant of joy! Her name is, in fact, Joy! She is vulnerable, she is gentle, she is in every way an infant, a small child. I accept her, I Love her, I embrace her."

"When did you first start to gaze into the Fire?"

"I first began fire gazing when I was a small child. I would gaze into the Flame and something would just open within me, in the middle of my eyes! And then I would begin to see shapes! Then off I was into a subtle trance. I was only able to do it a few times, though, because my mother thought it was evil and she told me that it was evil. I, of course, do not have any wishes to do anything of an evil nature, so that was the very last time I did it. Back when I was a child, that is.

Today, I believe that there are various things we are told are evil, because they are actually a source of Power. There are people who do not want us to get in touch with our sources of Freedom and Sight. I am not saying that fire gazing is going to give people powers! But I am saying that if you are of the Fire, then fire gazing is simply of your nature, a Language that speaks to you, that communes with you! The Fire *will* speak to you, *if* you are of the Fire.

There is nothing wrong about *not* being of the Fire, I just want to take the time to say this. If you are of the Water, then do not try to be of the Fire. I am of the Fire and I once thought I was of the Water, but all of that freezing, hardening and the many waves, were just not attune with my nature and I struggled all the time. You must find *your* element. Not my element, not their element, but *your* element! I can promise anyone who reads these words, that if you are not of the Fire, then these words will do nothing for your benefit. In such a case, the only thing these words can do for your benefit is to open you up to the possibility that you are of a different element, then you must go and find it."

"What does one gain and what can one benefit, from gazing into a flame?"

"The benefits of fire gazing are immense. If you want to gain complete control of the comings and going of your mind— gaze into the flame on a candlestick. As the flame itself, so will your thoughts be, also. Unified into a single effervescent essence, entire and whole of itself and yet still capable of swaying and bowing and rising according to your breath and the air around it. A single flame on a wick is controlled power; or, control *over* your Power. Both are essential for your mind. Though, none of this will work for you if you are not made of the Flame. If you are of another element, then something else will serve you well, not this. Find that which is of your own nature, do not be enticed by what is not.

While gazing into the flame, the long-forgotten memories and the deceptive illusions that have misled you will be brought to the forefront of your mind, right where you can see them plainly. The memories will be resurfaced, the illusions will be made transparent, you will be able to SEE. You may declare them as no more, you may decree justice over moments of injustice, you may claim victory over enemies in the past, you may bind on Earth as it is in Heaven and loose on Earth as is loosed in Heaven. But the Fire will not serve you if you are not of it. The Fire will only serve you if you *are* of it. If you are not of it, then you must seek answers elsewhere, not from me. Because I am the Fire and Flame is to Flame.

Fire gazing, to a Fire Gazer, is food to an empty stomach and then so much more. I was born anew when I gazed into the Flame. I was born a second birth when the Flame called out my name.

The Flame will calm and comfort an angry mind, will show you exactly how to control anger, power and disappointment. The Fire will comfort you at all times that you need comforting and shepherd you at all times when you need shepherding. You need not fear that the Flame will leave you, for it is always with you and will never leave you. Wherever you can light a Fire, there will the Flame be. Even when you cannot see the Fire, it is there with you, all you need to do is light a candle.

The Fire will not only remind you of what needs to be resurfaced in order to be overcome, but the Flame will also remind you of what needs to be brought back to mind in order to remember goodness long forgotten. We often have so much goodness that we have overlooked or forgotten to hold onto. Beauty, Good Luck, Happiness— these Treasures are like a Pink String that continually sews its way through every day of our lives and every hour, every moment of each day; this Pink String is unbreakable, unfettered and untangled. It is there, bearing Magic for us. Sometimes, we let go of the String and get lost wading in muddy ponds of misery, of disappointment and doubt. We lose sight of the String too easily; nevertheless, it is there! We only need to turn our faces to look at it, then to hold onto it. You will find that the Pink String weaving its way through your life, is capable of pulling you up and over the fraudulent ponds, the murky waters. The Flame reminds you of your Pink String when you need to be reminded of it. The Flame teaches you to reach out your hand and hold onto it, too. Th Pink String of Joy, Beauty, Good Luck, Lightheartedness— this takes up only a short time of our discussion, but I want you to remember the image of this String around your wrist, long after this conversation is over.

Anyone can be of the Fire, regardless of colour of the skin or of gender. The nature of a Fire Gazer is determined by one's Creed, not by one's race or gender."

"Is it possible for a person to be of all the elements?"

"I am of all the elements, so I can say that yes, it is possible. But when I go home at the end of the day, I go home to a Temple of Fire. I am not speaking of Hell! I am speaking of Eternal Flame of Life. You can come from one Home and still belong to the other

Homes, to a degree. But when you lay your head down at night, you wish to sleep in the bed made in your own home. That's what it is like. Likewise, someone may have a home in Water and wish to come back to her bed every night, while still belonging to Air, Earth and Fire— to a degree!

Like I have repeatedly said, the Water once felt like home to me and to a great degree and for a long time, too. But it was the freezing and the removal from onself in order to wash away, that was not akin to me and caused me pain and struggling. Now, for someone inherently of the Water, I can imagine that those qualities would not cause them pain nor struggle."

"What does it even mean to be 'of the Fire' or 'of the Water'? What does that even mean, in the real world? Do you simply go about your day relating your actions to an element? Is that how it goes?"

"That is basically what it is, yes. I really cannot say if it is the same for others, it's probably not, but that is basically how it is for me, yes. On the other hand, I *do* think that it is also this way for others. We see people with an affinity to the ocean, to lightning, to mountains and streams… many people take affinity to certain elements in nature. The difference is that they think nothing else of it, they only experience all of that in the Outer Flame aspect, in the exoteric aspect. They don't go into the Inner Flame and begin to carry an element (or the virtues of an element) with them, every day and every night. Again, it is the very same principle that entails some will penetrate deeper while others will linger on the outside of a thing. Some will step into a Cathedral and see chairs, pews and pillars. Others will step into a Cathedral and see carvings on the walls, take pictures of the carvings, then try to find their meanings. It is all a matter of where one clings: either onto the outside of a thing or onto the inside of a thing.

There is a concept that I have learnt from a very old manuscript. However, I am not allowed to mention it, because not everyone is supposed to read it. But I will say, that the concept I learned, is that those whose souls easily cling to the outer of a thing, also scatter their souls onto the surface of things, thinning their souls out, feeling what is not beneficial to oneself. Such individuals are easily offended. Meanwhile, there are yet others who immediately penetrate into the inner core of a thing (as I discussed with you earlier), able to extract from it what is beneficial to itself, thus maintaining vitality. This type of soul is not thinned out and is not easily offended. This type of soul can be classified as Neutral: not forming an opinion, but only diving into the object to extract what is beneficial to itself.

I am simply reminded of what I read in that manuscript, that is all. This is to reaffirm the notion that yes, I *do* walk around carrying my affinity to my Element and carrying it with me every day and every night, while others are just vaguely aware that they like to visit the beach, for example.

Others may perchance develop the ability to also penetrate into the inner area of a thing without their souls being scattered atop it, but such a practice would require full focus into the development of this ability, a full devotion and dedication."

"My thoughts now turn to the smoke, what is to be said of the smoke that the flame produces? What is smoke and what can it teach us? Or, what does smoke mean? Does it have a meaning all on its own?"

"Smoke is beautiful, it is something that only fire can create and it is a part of the air! Smoke is fire's lightest ally and it releases itself into the air, becoming one with it! Smoke dances just how fire dances; you will notice the qualities of smoke and fire are so alike. Smoke is the physical manifestation of the marriage of fire and air. In a few moments after you blow out your candle, the fire and air are in the ceremony, evident in the smoke that curls and dances and forms itself into many symbols onto the air. The ceremony lasts only a short while and then fire and air have become one; indistinguishable one from the other. Perhaps it is not even a ceremony; maybe it is the art and act of making love. The fire makes love to the air and it is the physical form of the smoke that proves it.

When Fire makes Love to the Air, this reminds us that Fire is *always* there; even when we cannot see it! This, in turn, comforts us, because Fire is Eternal and this is made evident in its Smoke. Even when we cannot see Fire, it is ready to reappear in an instant. Even when we cannot see the Hands that protect us, guide us, comfort us, soothe us— those Hands are certainly there, they are ready to reappear in an instant!

I am not against anyone who wishes to be religious and to practice a religion. I am only against how that type of passion moves in this world. It moves to divide and when in the wrong hands— even to destroy! I am not in favour of destruction. Furthermore, I believe in my heart that the original religion is the Religion of Fire. When did man first become conscious of the possibility of there being a Higher Being, a Supreme Being? I believe this first ignited along with man's discovery of fire in primordial, prehistoric times. When man discovered fire for the first time, man also discovered his conscious awareness and wonder for a Supreme Being, a Supreme Presence.

What was this substance that was hot and which danced? What was this material that brought warmth and provided meals? What was this burning light that could guide the eyes in the midst of darkness and lead the way towards more light? What was this thing that could scare away dangerous animals and frighten away hostile people?

When people discovered fire, people began looking for God. And I believe they found God actually in the Fire. The voice of God, the attributes of God; and they found the concept of Trust and Protection. I believe that Fire is the original, primordial, prehistoric conception of religion. The religion that man had not yet built ideas upon, had not yet placed new concepts upon, had not yet burdened with precedents and rules. The religion before religion was a concept— that is Fire. That was Fire, that still is Fire and that will always be — Fire!

What type of sin did the prehistoric fire separate people from? It was very simple. Fire separated people from those who wished to steal and to kill. Fire was the weapon of choice. Sin was not all the descriptions that people have for sin nowadays; rather, it was simple. If you wanted to hurt me, if you wanted to steal from me, then I would burn you with fire! Very simple. Entirely primordial. Before the hands of man had the chance of grabbing it and forming it into what it has become today. Today, people will hurt other people if they believe those other people are sinning! And so we have it, that in our modern day and age, the original sin has become the method of correcting those who are perceived as sinful! What twisted type of reality are we living in, today?

Of course, this is not to say that we must not punish those who harm others. We must in fact punish those who hurt others. But people need to be hurt because they first hurt others; not because they are perceived to be sinners for being different or for living differently. When a man wishes to harm another— the Fire must come in between him and his victim, in order to protect the one and to burn the other. Fire must be the separation between those who wish to harm and those whom they wish to harm. Burn the one who wants to hurt you. But do not hurt others when they do not wish to harm you.

If we were all to see our religion as Fire and if we were all to see sin as the primeval equivalents of sin, can you imagine how much peace we would have int this world?

I am not telling you to leave your religions and I am not telling you to adapt my own beliefs. I am not even telling you that you need to believe me. But if you were to believe the things I say, I do feel that you would be one more person Alive and Free! And I would like to see more persons Alive and Free. This still doesn't mean that if you do not believe in all the things that I have shown you and shared with you, that you will never be Alive and Free. It doesn't mean that. You may become Alive and Free through other ways. But I am saying that if you would like to try my Path, you are welcome to.

My Path does not defame any religion on Earth, it does not mock any religion on the planet. Because my path is primeval, it existed before all existed. It is innocent, it is antediluvian, it is forgotten but it is gradually being remembered today. My path is Innocence. And all are welcome to try Innocence.

I am only a child and perhaps all of the things I say are only childlike dreams and guesses. I am only a child and perchance all that I write are only childlike beliefs and behaviours. I am only a child and peradventure this conversation is but a figment of my own reality. I am only a child, notwithstanding, here you are— you listen and you ask, you believe and you question. You are comforted, you find Truths. You find Truths as one finds seashells on a seashore: just like a child! If it is not worthy, then why are you here? If it is not meaningful, then why do you sit with me and talk with me? It is possibly only my reality, but the Beauty in that is the fact that I have shared what is mine with you! You may keep what you find, if you want to. But you don't have to want to! You may do whatever you wish with it, just don't throw it away."

"Is it therefore, fair to say, that Dragons are the protectors of Innocence?"

"When you study the dragon in folklore, you will see that the dragon only allows the pure of heart access to its treasures. Likewise, Dragons are Keepers of Treasures that may only be accessed by the Pure of Heart. What is Purity of Heart? It is indeed Innocence. Therefore, you have understood well. Dragons are protectors of Innocence, the Innocent, the Pure of Heart. Dragons are also Keepers of Treasures that may only be accessed by the Pure of Heart.

I keep these Treasures and I teach them to you because I am Dragon and you are Pure of Heart. I hide these Treasures from those who ought not to find them, because I am Dragon and they are not Pure of Heart. The impure will not be able to understand anything I have written here, I have made certain of that. If you have read here what I have written and you understand well in the absence of overwhelming confusion, then you are Pure of Heart. An overwhelming confusion will overcome those who are not meant to have these Treasures. I am Dragon, so I have seen to it that this be so."

"Do you know what else I have noticed about the dragon of folklore?"

"What is it?"

"I can recount from my memories of stories, how the dragon of folklore is always guarding precious stones, mountains of gold coins, silver, rubies, precious metals and golden boxes... all manner of wealth and even varieties of magic, are all guarded by the dragon. You have mentioned the word 'treasures' often throughout our conversation and I know that you are pertaining to Treasures of the Soul and of the Otherworlds, of the Sister Realms and of the Skies and the Heavens, but I am now curious, how about the corporeal treasures of prosperity and wealth? Are these important? How important are they? Tell me!"

"I am so glad that you have asked this. The corporeal Treasures of Wealth and Prosperity; of precious metals and valuable stones, all of these are physically manifested vibrations and they are extremely valuable due to the nature of the energies that have produced them. Wealth is the fruit of the Tree of Dedication. Prosperity is the fruit of the Tree of Life. Life is meant to be lived not in poverty nor in hardship; but in prosperity and abundance. *That* is Life. Always anchor your roots into this Tree, never stray far from it. For without Prosperity, life on this planet becomes difficult. They will tell you that there is much 'beauty' to be had in hardship and difficulty, it is misleading and it would mean to lead you astray, but nay, hold fast onto Prosperity and stray not far from Wealth! For these are Treasures much needed in this Life! And even in the Lives to come.

The energies of Dedication produce the vibrations of Wealth. There is phenomenal Beauty in the mere fact that Wealth is a fruit of an energy which you can actually hold in your hands, trade with, work with, produce movement with! The thrill of Wealth— the actual thrill of it— lies in this fact. Wealth is a material form of Magic, or I could say, Wealth is, in actuality, the form of Magic which you can touch with your skin and work within the corporeal realm (the real world, the one we call the lower realm that we live in).

As to all things, there are distractions, there are misleadings, deceptions and fake versions of the Genuine, of the True. The true thrill of Wealth is not what you see displayed by useless actions of misled people. But a true thrill of Wealth will lift your Soul up to lofts, cliffs, heights, levels and heavens not previously reached before! Wealth and Prosperity are essences of the Soul and they do not pull or detract from the Stuff of the Soul; unlike what is popularly believed. Nay, on the contrary, a surge of Wealth is capable of branding you with a very strong set of Wings with which your Soul may fly Higher than it ever has flown before!

As always, there is an Inner and an Outer, there is an Inner World and an Outer World. As with everything else, we may view the face of Wealth in its Inner Form or we may view the face of Wealth in its Outer Form. To stand on the Inside and witness its Inner Face, is to stand and to witness one of the most beautiful existences that there is. A face luminescent, pearlescent and delightful! One that opens like a window allowing the rays of an Inner Heart to shine forth! A face smiling, uncontaminated by the ills and the misfortunes of this world. A face that unites all who look upon it, immediately and suddenly. A face that calls everyone home at the end of the day, to rooms that are warm, lit and filled with people who love you and who love one another. I believe that it can always be this way— every single minute of every single day!

Those who are only able to see the Outer Form of Wealth, see only the shadow of the actual person. A shadow only lurks behind the person who stands there, it is something that is of no value, cast upon a wall or the ground. That is the only face that most see when they look upon Wealth. It is also the only face that many experience when they accept Wealth into their lives. In both cases, it is such a pity. They squander, they are never truly satisfied, they envy, they fight, they are filled with greed... greed is born by the lack of comfort. One may have every comfort that others could imagine, but still have no comfort in one's own soul, in such a case, greed abounds! Greedy individuals are searching for the Inner Form of Wealth. They search and search, they cannot seem to find it. It is a face they faintly remember from somewhere... yet all the money in the world can't seem to lead them back to that familiar Warmth. The greedy seek the Flame, but they do not know it and it is in their unknowingness that they covet what others have, they covet more and more. They have a faint memory of the Fire, they cannot seem to find it, Wealth has become the closest thing to it that they can find. Like the man who has stumbled upon the cave of treasures and found all of the treasures in the world and yet, there is no candle burning in that cave, there is no light, there is no fire, there is no Magic. It is the shadow cave. The real Cave of Treasures is standing somewhere above, and they find themselves in the shadow cave that is but a dark illusion cast by the real image which is elsewhere.

Today we see many people ridiculing Wealth, brandishing it as undesirable, as corruptible and deceptive, so on and so forth. They are judging but the shadow of the true face of Wealth. If they could see Wealth in her Inner Form, they would judge it not."

"Why is it that we are taught, that Prosperity and Wealth are corrosions to the Soul of man and woman?"

“As usual, the people are not normally capable of placing the same amount of value upon the corporeal as they do on the incorporeal; upon the flesh and they do for the soul. The people tend to favour one over the other and magnify and uplift one to the downfall of the other. We see ‘enlightened ones’ who refuse food and water, in order to sit in one place and meditate for decades; we are witness to those who refuse to wear varieties of clothing, refuse to eat varieties of food, choose to live celibate and aloof on top of a mountain; in this world we bear witness to many forms of ignorance. What is fascinating, is that it is usually those who take so much joy in saying that others are ‘ignorant’, who are themselves ignorant. At the end of the day, they are *all* ignorant. What a circus!

Without a Soul, the physical Body has no Life and without a physical Body, the Soul has no Destiny. A soul cannot fulfill its Destiny once the body is deceased. A body cannot go on living when the soul has departed from it. The Soul and the Body are in need of one another, neither is more important than the other in your lifetime on this planet. Albeit, the Soul grants gifts to the Body which the Body cannot give itself on its own; however, the Body does the same for the Soul!

The happiness of eating an ice cream cone is a healing balm of delightful innocence for the Soul, an experience which would not be had if not for the human tongue! Sexual intercourse, the experience of touching another's skin, the simple delight of picking flowers, of frolicking in the sea and climbing a tree... these are gifts that the Body gives to the Soul. Truly, the Soul gives more gifts to the Body, as the Inner is always more capable than the Outer; for this is the way the Inner and Outer interact and are reflected in all walks and at all turns in Life. Nonetheless, the Outer is not less important than the Inner. The three Outer Layers of the Flame are not less important than the three Inner Layers of It. To extinguish the Outer is to extinguish the Inner. Albeit, the Inner Form of all things is Eternal, therefore, it shall undoubtedly find its way back into existence. But in relation to our precious gift of a Life that we are given to Live on this Earth, to extinguish the Outer is indeed to extinguish the Inner.

You are taught and they are taught, that Prosperity and Wealth do nothing for the Soul of man aside from malaligning it, because those who teach you are themselves malaligned. Wealth and Prosperity give *so* much to the Soul, that I go so far as to say that there are certain enslavements that even Magic Itself cannot conquer whilst ravaged by the vile hands of poverty. Magic can do all things— but listen here— when suffering in poverty, the first course of Magic is to escape the decaying fingers of poverty. What can you do whilst in poverty? You can barely do any good for your Body nor for your own Soul. You can barely do any good for anyone else, either! Not for yourself, your family, friends, or anybody else!

Magic Itself cannot conquer the need to escape poverty, as such, the first action of Magic is to release the Mage from the hands of poverty, only then may all other endeavours be taken.

Prosperity and Wealth are healing balms to the Soul. Money is a healing balm to families, relationships, friendships and whole nations of people. They will tell you that money does not heal, it is true that money does not heal those who have wounds that money cannot heal. It is very simple, it is not even profound. To every type of illness, to every type of wound, there is a specific ointment. You may not apply the ointment for the toes onto the eyes; you may not apply the ointment for the knee onto the tongue. For every ailment, there is a specific medicine. Money will not heal what it cannot heal. Very simple! And yet people romanticize this very practical fact. The other side of this same coin is that money will, in fact, heal the wounds that it *can* in fact heal!

For every ailment of man, there is a corresponding energy that is capable of bringing healing to the area. Be it of the Body or of the Soul.

Remember that Wealth is a vibration, it is an energy. Money is a vibration and an energy that heals what it is supposed to heal. Not to mention the fact that with Money, you are empowered to actually pay for medications that you could not have previously afforded, pay for treatments that you could not have previously paid for. That is another very practical fact.

There is a body of people who work to abolish money, altogether. They say that it never needed to exist and that it should never exist. A moneyless utopian world is what they desire. I do not mock their desires, I will not even say that their vision is not doable. But I will ask this: from whence are these desires born? Are these desires born from benevolence or from envy? Are their desires born from an understanding of nature, or in reality, are their desires born from the absolute misunderstanding of nature? From whence are the desires born? *That* is what I ask.

Their argument is, in fact, doable. It is a possibility to transform current society into a future moneyless utopian society where the value and the worth of everyone is measured only by their character traits. Possible. But then I ask this question: in such a society, will the character traits of those same people who envisioned this new world, in fact, be of any value to anyone? And that is a very important question to ask oneself. In the event that the character of the dreamer in such a society proves to be useless, of utterly no importance, then what will his next big dream be? Then how would such a person buy and sell based upon a character proven to be worthless in such a society? Furthermore, if all people knew that their character would be the factor empowering them to buy and to sell, would their expressed characteristics be genuine or would those expressed characteristics be only for show? Would people end up living with two faces as a result? There are many questions to be raised regarding this dream that some people have."

"Where does money derive its value from? When exactly can I know that what I have is valuable or not valuable? It looks like the value of money is not in the amount, itself; rather, it appears to be that the value of money is both physical *and* spiritual. When something is both physical and spiritual, how do I know if what I have is of definitive value or not?"

"Do you remember the parable in the Bible? The one of the rich man and the ageing widow with merely two copper coins? Who gave money of more value? The rich man who could easily give much or the poor widow who gave all that she could give? The value of the poor woman's two small coins was greater than the value of the rich man's many offered coins. Why is this so? This is because the value of money comes from who is giving it rather than from the physicality of the material object, itself. Furthermore, the one who loves you more will always give you more value than the one who loves you less, regardless of the amount that is given. The value of the Love definitely weighs more heavily than the value of the coins. They who do not know this are blinded to a powerful truth."

"I sincerely understand all that you have explained to me and I can now clearly see all the ways that I have previously been misled. Thank you *so* very much for what you are giving to me!

But I still want to know more. I would like to know, what is to be said about those who have not worked a day in their lives and yet they are at want for no good thing? What is to be said about those who eat of the good fruits of the tree that they did not plant or that they did not even harvest the fruit thereof?"

"Many receive the Fruit without working the initial energies. We see this in generations of families who are wealthy and privileged, yet who have not lifted a finger to create any of that wealth that we can see. And so what? If you could collect precious stones and metals, fill your treasure chests with your valuable assets and then hide those treasure chests in your cave, would you not make your cave accessible to your family? Love, Family, Relationships— *these* are the most important, fundamental aspects of the Dragon Creed. A Dragon does not hoard for himself alone, but also for his bloodline and for those whom he Loves. It is not a mistake, it is not a sin, that we see those who inherit the caves that others built before them, that others have guarded for them. In fact, it is to be expected that caves will be shared with those whom they were meant to be shared.

Do not have that bitter taste in your mouth when you see Wealth walking amongst those whom you have judged unworthy of her. If they have since made themselves unworthy through their own negative actions and their own negative mindsets, then that is between them and the Flame. Stop to ask yourself first, if you yourself are not being negative in making judgments of them. In the meantime, it is not worth having a bitter taste in your mouth over the fortunes or the misfortunes of others. The Soul that does not cling to the surface of a thing, is the Soul of the Immortal Being.

Observe the Dragon of Legend. He guards a Treasure, she guards a Treasure. It has oft been mistold, in saying that Dragons guard treasures of Kings. Nay, but it is the King who seeks out the Dragon. The Dragon guards only what is his or her own."

"I would like to know, what is the medicine to counteract the effects of greed? What is the healing balm that should be applied to greed?"

"Greed is counteracted by True Love. True Love can lead one to the Flame! The greedy may be led to the Flame through the Heart of True Love. Love brings comfort, brings warmth, brings home, brings virtue, brings the True Face of Wealth along with it. Love is a very powerful vibration, a magnificent and magnanimous energy! The unloved become greedy. They were never Truly Loved. That is why greed can be found both in the heart of the poor man and in the heart of the rich man. Because all men— rich and poor— may be an unloved man.

Of course, I am not saying that we must all go around offering 'true love' to the greedy individuals. Rather, we must all see that everything begins at home, in the act of Truly Loving those who have been given to us to Truly Love. If you want to counteract greed in the world, do not think that picking up placards and pitchforks is going to chase the big bad men of Wallstreet away! To uproot a thing, one must pull out the very root of it, not merely attempt to hack away the stems or the branches with a pair of scissors. Love all those who are given to you to Love. Love your family and Love your own Soul. Especially the other half of your own Soul. This is how you counteract greed. Provide for them, never allow them to be of want for any good thing. Of course, there are times when we wish to be able to do this but we cannot; in such cases, walk through difficulties alongside them hand-in-hand, always striving and always fighting to make sure that they know and feel that you are going through your hardships together and that one day you will surely come out of it, still together, and this time Victorious!"

"Is this world truly a 'lower realm' as you have described it?"

"This world that we live in is merely a single, pearlescent, glittery marble on the floor upon where I sit at the feet of my father. Upon that floor, there are many marbles that I may pick up and play with. My father sits on the armchair in that room and I sit on the floor at his feet, as all children love to do while playing with toys in the comfort and protection of one's own home, where one is loved and cherished. This world that we live in now is but a single pretty marble on that floor. Actually, this world is but one planet in the universe— the universe being that single marble. There are other marbles strewn all over that floor, they are other universes and they contain their own planets and stars, galaxies and solar systems.

Our time on Earth is but a time to learn and to love. To learn what Love is. And to learn how to love and to learn to keep it. A time to practice Magic, a time to construct and to take down. A time to laugh and to learn how to laugh even louder. We have fought battles great and small, then we won them all. To return to my father's house and sit on the floor at his feet, is to return to my home, where I hold this marble in my hand and remember the many comings and goings contained within it. The marble is pearlescent, glittery, with swirls of shiny colours in it, a lovely little marble; I am not surprised why I wanted to go inside it, it is not hard to want to jump inside a pretty marble like this one."

"Are there other worlds within this marble that we now share? Other worlds that we just don't see, that we are unaware of?"

"When the soul of man attaches to the surface of things, the remaining soul that is intact is left thin and blunt, unable to penetrate the veils that flow between worlds within this world. Yes, the other worlds are there/ are here, but very few individuals are able to penetrate them, to perceive them. The veils were once lifted, but later reinstated when mankind proved itself to be cruel to the other sides, insensitive of their natures."

"Is it possible for the different marbles on the floor to bump into one another, to collide? Can they bounce on and off of one another?"

"Yes, and this is called Chaos. Sometimes, the marbles may even exchange their pearlescent swirls and glittery patterns. Other times, you may walk in and out of multiple marbles at the same time. This is all called Chaos. I told you that Chaos is not the same thing as the 'chaos' word in the dictionary. Peradventure it has the same technical meaning; nonetheless, Chaos is the Inner Face while chaos is the Outer Face. To handle Chaos is to handle the comings and goings of worlds."

"Are there certain difficulties that arise from the handling of Chaos? I can only imagine that to hold such a thing in one's hand, would be akin to holding a burning fire in your palm. Anything but easy and many possible troubles could arise."

"You have thought well. There are indeed difficulties and they are great."

"Tell them to me, I would like to hear, I would like to understand what it is like."

"Sometimes, I lose track of past, present and future. Then due to my impatience with the annoying attributes that people have, I can then lose track of the improvements I have made in certain relationships, lose track of feelings I have developed or feelings I have already worked on... the frightening part is when I lose track overnight. I can go to sleep and wake up the next morning unable to pick up where I left off the day before, because I have found myself somewhere in the future and sometimes somewhere in the past. These are difficulties that are remedied through Fire Gazing. Fire Gazing has done for me, more than what anything else has done for me.

I am also unable to speak in mundane terms. I am able to speak only either as a small child or through complicated, coded symbolism. Not everyone understands the small child and not everyone understands the semiotician. But for you, I am able to take the semiotics and transform it into the talks of a small child. Or, I hope and strive to do so.

I care all and I care not at all. The ways of the minds of man bore me and in an instant, I care not at all. But then I care totally and completely, with no hints of giggly feelings in between. I Love as the Fire Loves, there is nothing funny about it. I either burn, or I am extinguished. But the Fire is teaching me to also dance, to sway, to bow and to rise. I am learning well how to be as the Fire— not only burn and not only be extinguished— something that knows the graceful ways that are in-between."

"Are there things that Dragons are unable to tolerate? Is there one thing that nobody should ever do or say to a Fire Keeper?"

"A Keeper of Fire is unable to tolerate being micromanaged in the mind. Many have attempted to micromanage me, especially men whom I have known, because such is the nature of men— to see a woman as just another part of his life that he needs to manage. It is not beneficial to those who attempt to micromanage me because I am aware of what they are doing, why they are doing it and what outcome they wish to have. Sometimes, I will play along with it, but most times, my Magic will not allow for me to be micromanaged.

Look here, I am not even saying that I do not allow myself to be practiced on and studied on like a project of some sorts. I am not above the abilities of other people to manipulate, to charm and to predesignate. I call it 'predesignation' when a person makes plans to lead someone else's mind towards a certain outcome that they have calculated to be beneficial for themselves. I am not saying that I am above predesignation capabilities of other individuals, but I am saying that my Magic is. The Aether that runs through my veins and that surrounds me, will not allow me to be blinded. Admittedly, I can sometimes be too keen and look too hardly into things (this is a fault of mine), but this is a weakness of mine which I am working on. But that is a different story. Right now, I am talking about my Magic. It will not allow me to be predesignated, because it is against the natural laws to micromanage what is greater than yourself. Should I be ashamed to say this? I think not. I can accept that those who have wished to micromanage me are not greater than me. Keepers of Fire cannot be predesignated, they cannot be manipulated, they cannot be led into a desired state. You cannot lure a Dragon into a cave. The caves belong to the Dragons, you will find yourself lost if you ever attempt to act as the Master in the presence of Dragons. You are not Master, not even the King is the Master. Only the Dragon knows its Magic, its Treasures, its caves.

The downside of this all, is that it takes the lightness and the surprise out of relationships. The

Magic becomes too severe and light happiness is lost. That is such an undesirable side effect. But it may be overcome, by allowing Magic to work without placing your own emotional states into it. Magic will defend you, look out for you and protect you. There is no need to get emotionally involved with the process. It is far more beneficial to retain Lightness of Being, to keep the Pink String in sight. But it is also wise that others not attempt to micromanage Keepers of the Flame."

"Are there other Dragons in the world? Are there many of us?"

"You may have noticed that the dragons of folklore are far in between and often fly alone. This is also the case with Dragons in Spirit. We are far in between and we fly alone unless we have found another Dragon to fly with. It is not that we do not want to find another! It is simply that there are very few of us to find. There are others, but many are sleeping. There are others, but many are afraid. There are others, but only a few believe.

I am the oldest person I know. I have never met anyone who feels older than me, I always feel older than anyone I ever meet. I am the youngest person I know. I have never felt older than any of the children that I ever meet. The only people I meet who feel as childlike as I feel, are the little children. But then those little children grow up! It is because I am the oldest, that I am able to be the youngest. It is because I am the youngest, that I am the oldest. It is because of these two facts that I often feel alone in this world, it is arduous to find another. I am wary of people and I grow tired of how their minds work; I grow impatient of their doubts, fears and cowardice. They are not childlike but they are childish. They are not mature but they are old. I am mature and not old. I am childlike and not childish. How often is one like me found? How very scarce is my species? I was invoked into flesh by Magic and I am shrouded in Magic all of my days! Without my Magic, my atoms become like fluid, they spread out across things and pieces of me are left all around. My Magic binds my

Soul to my Flesh and my Flesh to my bones. How often can you find one like me? How scarce is my species? I am of the Day and because I am of the Day, this means I am Master of the Night. Because I am Day, I am Night and because I am Night, I am Day. Tell me, when have you met another like me? Will you ever meet another like me?

I do not say that I am a Dragon person with Dragon wings and Dragon's breath! But as I say, 'I am Master of Fire', I may also say, 'I am Dragon'. This is to give Life to what I am saying, to give Life to the fact that I am Keeper of Treasures and Viewer of Hearts. This is not to say that I have reptilian blood running through my veins; I do not believe in such a thing. Others do, but I do not.

The physical manifestation of a Dragon is not as a person, rather, of a shapeshifter. Chaos Dragons come from Chaos— not chaos as we know the word to be— but Chaos as the place of possibilities, of Darkness, of the absence of time, space, relativity and all known laws of physics. The eagle flying above you could be your Dragon. The Dragonfly always landing on your window could be your Dragon. In its original form, its power is so immense that it will paralyse you, that is why it prefers to show itself in other forms that will not frighten you. I suppose, that to be guarded and raised by Dragons is to be *of* the Dragons. Then one may say, 'I am Dragon'. At the same time, this is *not* to say that 'being Dragon' is everything in life. It is not something that ought to consume every nook and cranny of your life; rather, it is the actions of the Dragon that ought to consume every nook and cranny of your life. What are the actions of the Dragon? To master Fire, to understand the Flame, to live by the Creed— these are the actions to keep. To be called something and to obsess over being called something is not fruitful. To actually act like something is fruitful. To actually embody a good thing is fruitful.

To keep the Treasures, to understand the Flame, to live by the Creed— this is to be Dragon. Guard your Innocence, walk in your Purity of Heart, learn the Language of the Fire, return to the antediluvian Path. It is time for Dragons to awake, it is time for Gods to roam this Earth again. It is time for Beauty to overcome evil; not through naivete, but through the Beautiful Strength of the Fire, of the Dragon. The mortals have had their reign. It is now time to take back what is ours."

Stamvalinvader Grolovskovelo Seniamentodragon Kalihandere Arindinggomar Velechuske Montehielo

End

"God is one and eternally unchangeable. He reigns over all. The gods are diverse and innumerable, for Divinity is eternal and infinite. The greatest gods are the souls of constellations. Each constellation has its own suns and stars, earths and moons, and all issues from the celestial Fire of Zeus, from the Initial Light. Half-conscious, inaccessible and unchangeable, they govern the mighty whole by their unvarying movements. Each revolving constellation draws along in its ethereal sphere phalanxes of demi-gods or radiant souls who were formerly human, and who, after descending the scale of kingdoms, have gloriously ascended the cycles, and finally issued from the round of generations. It is through these divine spirits that God breathes, acts, and manifests Himself; or, rather, these form the breath of His living soul, the rays of His eternal consciousness. They rule over

armies of lower spirits which govern the elements; they control the universe. Far and near, they surround us, and, although of immortal essence, they assume ever-changing forms, according to nation, epoch or region...
I struggled to find them, braved death, and, as is said, descended into hell to tame the demons of the abyss, to summon the gods from on high to my beloved Greece, that lofty heaven might unite with earth, listening with delight to strains divine. Celestial beauty will become incarnate in the flesh of woman, the Fire of Zeus will run in the flesh of woman, the Fire of Zeus will run in the blood of heroes, and, long before mounting to the constellations, the sons of God with shine forth like Immortals."

— *Orpheus*

SPECIAL MENTIONS

I had a new copyeditor this time around since my usual copyeditor, Toula Fanariotou, was harvesting peaches during the editing period of this manuscript. Toula has a peach farm! She harvests peaches every peach season along with her husband, George, in Greece. To take her place, I had Priyanka Dass jump in on the responsibility. Priyanka is a biotechnologist and writer who lives in India. She is a remarkable woman who loves children (she babysits for a French family in India) and who is devoted to her relationship with God. She was on my beta team for *The Conversation of Venusta* and she is still on my beta team now, the only difference is that this time around she also played the role of copyeditor. I thank her for her time and devotion to copyediting the manuscript for me.

I thank everyone on my beta reader team who has stepped up to the responsibility of writing a review for this work. I thank them for their time and dedication. I also thank them for the genuine friendship that they have extended to one another and to me.

I am above all, thankful to the Spirit Dragons who have protected, taught and guided me on my own journey of Fire. Most especially to the one who has been with me since my birth. Valem, valem.

I am so thankful for and appreciative of, the work of * Jim Crotty, who is not only a part of my beta reader team, but who also collaborated with me for the cover of this book. Jim is a professional photographer who so often captures the beauty of nature through his lens. He was also responsible for the book cover of *The Conversation of Venusta*. Jim easily captures my vision and effectively interprets it through his camera.

I initially planned to be on the cover of this book, myself! I had a vision of myself on the cover of my own book where I would interpret the soul of it. I contacted a fashion designer friend who was eager to send me his gowns to wear for the photoshoot and I scouted around for a holiday vacation I could take somewhere off in a log cabin in the woods around some steep cliffs. The only problem was the photographer. How was I supposed to book a photographer on holiday? So, I figured I would be my own photographer via tripod! Eventually, after realising that the task at hand would require so much extra thought and extra stress, I decided it was time to change my vision and work with Jim once again. The result of our second collaboration is stunning and I am just thankful that I have his expertise and eagerness right within my reach!

Lastly, but not the least, I thank *you* who holds this book in your hands. Thank you for embarking bravely upon this journey, thank you for courageously walking the Path and thank you for seeing yourself through to the end. I welcome you, Fire Keeper!

* Please visit Jim Crotty and check out his work: www.jimcrotty.com; https://500px.com/jimcrotty

The main typeface in this book is set in 12 pt. *Perpetua*, by Eric Gill (1882- 1940), who was a British sculptor and stonecutter named *Royal Designer for Industry* by the *Royal Society of Arts* in London. The font itself was crafted in such a way, as to resemble hand-chiseled engravings, hence, who better to create such a feel for a font, than a sculptor and stonecutter?

"Perpetua may be judged in the small sizes to have achieved the object of providing a distinguished form for a distinguished text; and, in the large sizes, a noble, monumental appearance."
~ Stanley Morison

Printed in Great Britain
by Amazon

79479702R00185